Soul Sunday gives parents all over the world a way to understand each other by learning about religious differences. Tolerance and respect for such differences will help lead us to peace.

> —Muhammad D. Yusufu, former Inspector General,
> Minister of the Interior, and Member of the
> Supreme Military Council of Nigeria

Soul Sunday is a must read, not only for families, but for everyone who wishes to understand better the wonderful and diverse world we live in today. With her delightful and refreshing style, I look forward to more thoughtful words from Carrie Brown-Wolf in the future.

> —Pastor Bill Cox

Through her seminars and now through her book, **Soul Sunday**, Carrie Brown-Wolf is offering critically needed direction to religiously blended families yearning to make their homes spiritually whole. Within the family framework she helps us find the fruitful point where religious conviction and spiritual exploration can reinforce each other. Moreover, **Soul Sunday** does this by offering practical activities and projects for the family to do together. They can overcome whatever fear there may be of other world religions, and as the family members grow in knowledge, so too do they grow together.

> —Rabbi Richard Baroff

As a Lutheran pastor keenly interested in educating children in the inclusive teachings of Jesus, **Soul Sunday** provides just the kind of guidance I've been looking for.

> —Pastor Rich Mayfield, author of
> *Reconstructing Christianity*

As parents of two elementary school-aged children living abroad, my husband and I are constantly struggling with how to teach and maintain our Indian culture while learning about the cultures to which we are exposed daily in our host countries. Because there is no structured, organized course we can attend abroad, **Soul Sunday** *will be the perfect tool for us to share and openly discuss information about topics we hear about.* **Soul Sunday** *should be required reading for not only expatriate families, but all families interested in learning about the world and understanding their neighbors.*

—Hina Pandya, M.D.

Soul Sunday *is a unique tool that provides a forum for families to discuss spiritual, moral, and ethical issues outside the confines of formalized religion. Learning about the observances of different religions and cultures can facilitate meaningful dialogue about what matters to families and why.* **Soul Sunday** *provides families with a framework to organize celebrations and rituals in a way that can work for each family.*

—Cassandra Wilson, L.C.S.W.

Carrie Brown-Wolf has spent her life teaching young people about the values of diversity and the richness of multicultural awareness and attitudes. She also knows what types of activities and projects engage children and make learning fun. **Soul Sunday** *is an inspiring book and has unique value for any family.*

—Jane Sanborn, Director of the Colorado Outdoor
Education Center and author of *Bag of Tricks*

Soul Sunday *is a welcome and wonderful tool for families striving to understand and live in a world of religious diversity, while strengthening their own religious heritage.*

—Martin I. Bresler J.D.,
Intergroup Relations Activist

Soul Sunday

Soul Sunday®

A Family's Guide
To Exploring Faith and Teaching Tolerance

Carrie Brown-Wolf

www.soulsunday.org
info@soulsunday.org

Published in the United States by:
TEO Summit Press
PO Box 23973
Silverthorne, CO 80498
970.262.7631

www.soulsunday.org
info@soulsunday.org

Library of Congress Control Number: 2007902307

Cover and interior design: Jennifer Lindstrom
Playshop artwork: Stacey Sattler
Author photograph: Kate Cosby

ISBN-13: 978-0-9791536-0-0
ISBN-10: 0-9791536-0-3

Printed in 2007

For Eleanor, Tennyson, and Olivia

With all my Heart

Acknowledgements

Creating an acknowledgements page is much like writing an Oscar acceptance speech. So many people are involved that one runs the risk of speaking well past the buzzer, or worse yet, forgetting someone. Writing *Soul Sunday* has truly been a compilation of my schooling, work and volunteer efforts, and has involved my friends, family, and spiritual mentors. I thank everyone involved.

Of course, the book could not have been conceived without the faithful partnership of my husband, Dan, or our three phenomenal kids, Eleanor, Tennyson, and Olivia. My deepest love and gratitude go out to them.

The support from my parents, siblings, and in-laws has certainly provided inspiration and relentless encouragement. I am deeply grateful for the friendship of my oldest and closest allies, and I would not be the person I am without the friends I depend on daily; you know who you are. I also thank my mentors, who have pushed me forward in life and provided me with great wisdom.

I appreciate all of you who read and re-read this book and helped carve it into shape. The making of *Soul Sunday* would not have happened without the terrific work and advice of Jenn Lindstrom, Stacey Sattler, Barbara Munson, and Martin Bresler. A special thank you to Andrea Clarkson for taking my hand and walking me through parts of the book where I did not want to go. Finally, I credit many of you who helped me critique and frame the artistic vision of *Soul Sunday*.

Thank you all for being the greatest part of my life!

Foreword

The world, which was created in six days, was a world without a soul. It was on the seventh day that the world was given a soul.
—Abraham Heschel, *The Sabbath*

"Who doth know the mind of God?"
—Saint Paul

Not so many years ago, the Sabbath—Sunday for some, Saturday for others, Friday for Muslims—was a day for rest and reflection, a day for family, a day for fun, a day for the soul. Now, for most of us, the idea of the Sabbath has been whittled down to an hour in church or temple. And even that hour seems to have little purpose for many.

When I listen to the conversations of parents, I hear common themes: "Kids these days don't have time to play," "Family time doesn't happen anymore...we're all too busy," "We barely sit down to eat together, let alone talk." Imagine if life were different. Imagine having a day, or just an hour or two, when life slowed down. When you could sit with your kids and talk about life and death, and right and wrong. Imagine a time each week to watch the clouds or listen to a stream, together. For me, the Sabbath isn't just a day; it's an idea. It can be a moment, a day, or a week. It's a time for reflection—time to stop the ordinary and examine the extraordinary. It's a time for the soul.

Soul Sunday offers parents a way to put the idea of Sabbath back into the lives of their families. For those of you who care about the moral lives of your children, it could be the most important parenting book on your shelf.

Soul Sunday began the way the best of practical books begin—with practice. It didn't come from theory, but from the experience and practice of one family and their effort to create a new kind of Sabbath. *Soul Sunday* is a workbook—full of practical ways to engage children in discovery and discussion. It's a book for parents who care about making things happen, about taking action to change their lives.

Many parents, most perhaps, come back to their faith when they have children. Even if we suffered through hours of boring Sunday school, filled with paper Jesus dolls, endless Christmas pageants, and tormenting confirmation classes, we know that spiritual education is important. At its best, religious school gives children a place to think about bigger questions: Why are we here? What are our responsibilities to others? Why is religion important? Why is there pain? What happens after death? With few exceptions, leaders at religious institutions educate from a single point of view, the view accepted by their faith.

Although most of us would say that the best educational practices offer multiple viewpoints and encourage children to form their own opinions, few of us carry this practice into church, synagogue, temple, or mosque. Why? Why don't the biggest mysteries deserve the deepest thought and broadest search? Why do we close our children off from other points of view when we come to questions of faith?

Soul Sunday offers parents a way to educate rather than preach. Its roots lie in the effort to bridge two religions in a single family. Its fruit is a gift for parents who want to help their children think deeply about the mysteries of life. *Soul Sunday* won't be for everyone. It won't appeal to those who "know" the right path. But for those parents who, like Paul, are open to the mystery of the mind of God, *Soul Sunday* is an important book.

—Scott Brown, author of *How to Negotiate with Kids* and
founding member of the Harvard Negotiation Project

Soul Sunday®

Part I:

Part II:

Playshops: Twenty seasonal hands-on spiritual sessions

Introduction

At our house, and most likely at yours, spiritual discussions have been left on the back burner as we have tried to squeeze more and more schoolwork, meetings, and plenty of activities into our weeks. As parents we don't always have the time to answer religious, philosophical, and spiritual questions satisfactorily. Our four year old has wondered many things like: Why is the sky blue? How does God hear? Why does Buddha have a belly? All of our children have asked important questions as they've heard about world-wide religious wars, hatred, prejudice, and suffering. Because my husband is Jewish, and I, Christian, we have a special need to explain both our faiths and to help our children develop their own personal identities. One day we hope they are able to find answers to spiritual questions and create a path to God on their own.

Soul Sunday grew out of the need to bring us together, as a family, to talk and understand, and to explore our faith. We wanted to create a specific time for questions, discussion, and voicing concerns. We designated Sunday evening to talk with our children about all things spiritual (and some things only generally spiritual). We have used activities to prompt discussions and have encouraged the children to stretch their imaginations. We have provided a theme and structure which usually has included cardboard, paints, yarn, glue, and other supplies. We have been amazed at what has developed: some of the most thought-provoking questions and powerful insights have occurred while sitting together on our kitchen floor! The results have been enormously rewarding, as each child has learned about faith, and also about the diversity of the world. Best of all, they have become more self-confident, introspective, and compassionate individuals.

This book provides instructions on creating your own *Soul Sunday* sessions and activities. Part I of *Soul Sunday* explores the need for families to connect and find faith together while creating a spiritual path to follow. This section helps raise awareness about major world religions—Hindu, Buddhist, Jewish, Christian, and Islamic—while encouraging families to build personal relationships with each other and with God.

Part II provides hands-on projects for families to do together during their *Soul Sundays*. Twenty Playshops are organized by season and involve activities that delve into and teach about faiths from around the world. The Playshops include activities with whimsical names like Dancing Diwali, Mind the Matzoh, Meditating Moments, and Hiking Hajj. They are hits with our kids.

The beauty of *Soul Sunday* is that the entire family gets involved…whether you have one child, or a handful. Grandparents are invited too.

I invite *your family* to try *Soul Sunday* and see for yourself what strides a family can take in the quest for faith, understanding, harmony, and peace.

—Carrie Brown-Wolf

Soul Sunday®

Part I

ONE

Why Can't God Make Me Spiderman?

If your Soul has no Sunday, it becomes an orphan.
—Albert Schweitzer

When my son, Tye, was four years old and full of sound effects and superhero actions, he desperately wanted to become Spiderman. My husband, Dan, and I bought him a costume for Halloween. It was good, Tye said, but it still didn't make him the real thing. We went to the library and checked out Spiderman stories. They were good, Tye said, but they still didn't make him fly. When he turned five his friends bought him web shooters. They were a bit better than good because they actually shot stuff, said Tye, but they didn't have real webs. We talked to him about his fantasy, but Tye told us he had already talked to God. He said he prayed every night to wake up and be Spiderman, but God wasn't listening.

How do we, as parents, explain to a child that no matter how hard and how earnestly he prays to God, he still won't wake with a webbed suit? How do we answer questions for ourselves as individuals? In our family we decided to create an environment to safely explore questions like these that life tossed our way. Because my husband and I were raised in different religious communities we have struggled with interfaith issues. We needed to find a safe forum for discussion of religious education outside of the synagogue and church. We chose to home-school our faith by incorporating our beliefs and common values, our appreciation for all cultures, and a desire to learn more. We named our immersion *Soul Sunday*.

Creating an environment for our three children to ask questions has opened many doors. We have explored religions, taught ethics, and gained a greater respect for different cultures. As a family we have learned about diversity and societies foreign to our own. Along the way, we have built a deeper faith in our convictions. We've smiled at our children's sincere questions and have done our best to help them understand the big questions in life. With a forum like *Soul Sunday*, we can be serious and silly while gaining our children's trust. We garner respect, build confidence, and develop faith for our kids.

Soul Sunday does involve a commitment. Our time with our children is typically consumed with soccer practice, dance lessons, homework, baseball, piano, computer games, chess, and cheerleading. We become as overwhelmed as our kids. Parents find themselves shuttling carpools and dishing out dinner while creating calendars that make Donald Trump's look elemental. Why do we do it? We want to give our children every opportunity. We want them to live with joy, challenge, and wisdom. However, we engage in so many activities that we often forget to slow down and realize the most important: creating a space and place for spiritual growth and family bonding.

Families need time together. While our culture has become obsessed with the immediate gratification of instant messaging and fast-food restaurants, we have lost the ability to take time to engage with each other. More than a century ago Mark Twain wrote in *The Innocents Abroad*:

In America we hurry, which is well; but when the day's work is done, we go on thinking of losses and gains, we plan for the morrow, we even carry our business cards to bed with us and toss and worry over them when we ought to be restoring our racked bodies and brains with sleep. We burn up our energies with these excitements and either die early or drop into a lean and mean old age at a time of life which they call a man's prime in Europe.…. What a robust people, what a nation of thinkers we might be if we would only lay ourselves on the shelves occasionally to renew our edges.[1]

Although Twain's observations were written long ago, not much has changed. Our society still has little time, and we continue to speed along without pausing to reflect and rest.

Finding time is complicated, yet it is well worth the effort to include *Soul Sunday* in monthly or weekly plans. It takes time to:

- Create relationships
- Answer questions
- Explore diversity
- Live well
- Love abundantly

Carving out a time for *Soul Sunday* can help families in many ways. Making it a weekly priority will achieve the best results, but if time is tight, begin with a monthly session and let the process grow. It is in the journey that families will discover spirituality.

In our family, *Soul Sunday* is a highly anticipated event. Dan and I have created rituals to keep expectations consistent. Not only does this create a sense of excitement and anticipation, but also, it makes the kids feel comfortable and secure. They know *Soul Sunday* is an organized time to listen, to learn, and to ask questions. They realize it is for them.

Organization of any event takes preparation. A meeting moves better if it is organized, especially when young children are involved. Before beginning the *Soul Sunday* adventure, Dan and I needed to lay the groundwork. To keep ourselves organized, we created a small corner in a closet for *Soul Sunday* materials. This specific space helped keep us better prepared.

We purchased Bibles, workbooks, and games. We looked up world religions at the library. I searched the Internet for activities on spirituality. We bought simple, plastic binders for the kids to fill with thoughts, prayers, notes, and lessons, and they made personal covers for them. Having something tangible has given the spiritual journey substance.

Soul Sunday is an activity we do almost every Sunday. Obviously, there are weekends we are away or busy with birthdays and holidays. However, on most Sundays we finish dinner, put on pajamas, and toss pillows on the floor. Sitting on pillows is still a novelty. The kids think it's lavish and decadent. We sit in a circle, hold hands, and sing silly songs. In our house, "Twinkle, Twinkle Little Star" has been sung so many times it deserves a Grammy. Although it may be corny, singing songs makes us all laugh. Laughing makes us feel closer. We have set the stage for bonding.

Once we have their attention we choose a theme or a lesson for the session. In addition to spirituality and religion, we discuss moral issues about friendships, bullies, and personal challenges. My husband and I will share simple experiences of our own, which opens the dialogue. We do this hoping the kids will share, and they do.

We have learned things about our kids during *Soul Sunday* that I'm glad I know.

When my oldest daughter, Ellie, was in first grade her aunt married her long-time lesbian partner. The couple, Laura and Cassie, no longer lives near us, but they have continued to play a pivotal role in our children's lives. Ellie loves them very much. She proudly went to school and told her friends about their secret elopement. What she wasn't prepared for were the accusations of blasphemy and wrongness thrown her way. She came home in tears.

We talked to her. Laura and Cassie talked to her. Her grandparents talked to her. We made *Soul Sunday* a time for acceptance and understanding that week. Whether you agree or not is not the issue. From this, Ellie came away with a strong conviction for love. "Why should it be bad to have more love in the world?" she asked.

Our kids have wrestled with questions about God, about death, about beliefs. Tears have been shed about sharing a new toy and meeting a new teacher. To develop a starting base that is relevant for our Judeo-Christian family, we sometimes relate these issues to Bible lessons. Later we connect these lessons to other people, social diversity, and various cultures. Our world has become an intimate gathering.

We talk about cultures, families around the world, poverty, politics, and peer pressure in addition to religion and spirituality. *Soul Sunday* gives us the time and the space to feel safe, to communicate, and to develop meaningful relationships. It has also opened doors for Dan and me. Not only have we strengthened bonds with our kids, but we have confronted our own faiths. We have questioned each other and ultimately have become more devoted to our own personal beliefs. I have read many books on religion, attended more than one study group, gotten involved in a local church, joined a yoga class, and participated in many community events. Dan also devotes much time to the community and has taken time to learn about different religions. Our relationship with each other has strengthened as we talk about difficult issues and decide how to share experiences with the kids.

After a discussion, *Soul Sunday* never finishes without a fun, hands-on project that develops our ideas and helps the kids understand the lesson. The activities vary from art and dramatic play to physical activities and games. Dan and I share experiences of our own, which helps the kids explore their spirituality. During one *Soul Sunday*, we all drew pictures of what God looked like to us. I told the kids that when I was a little girl sitting in Sunday school, I could not believe God had light brown hair, glowing skin, and perfect blue eyes. I recreated my drawing of God for my children. It was not a picture of a bearded man. Instead, I drew a floating, bloated, gray cloud. It was white in the middle, but was covered with ears: pink ears, brown ears, black and white ears. I wanted all our prayers "to be heard." The kids laughed with delight and satisfaction when they saw my drawing.

During *Soul Sunday* we often study about another country or region. We spin the globe, find the country, and launch into a creative, learning playtime to begin the session. After a discussion we color, bake, mold clay, or act out theatrical productions. We have fun as a family.

Soul Sunday closes with a prayer, a thank you, or just another song. Sometimes we quote from Scripture, other times, the Qur'an (Koran), or Hindu mystics. When we finish, our kids groan because we are done, and almost always ask if we can do it again the next night.

In his book, The *Soul of the Child*, Michael Gurian explains the critical importance of raising spiritual children. He says, "Studies continually reveal that children who are raised in a spiritual or religious path show greater levels of happiness than children who have little or no religion in their lives; studies show them to demonstrate fewer behavioral problems and to engage in greater moral behavior. Religion (spiritual life) is a cornerstone of raising healthy children."[2] Creating the space and finding the time to do a *Soul Sunday* will build spirituality, confidence, and relationships. It should be kept simple and structured, fun and yet meaningful. *Soul Sunday* is the time to learn about faith, and serve as a forum that is creative as well as insightful.

Most of us realize that kids often lose their focus. Children have curious questions and short attention spans. In the beginning, my kids became obsessed with using the hole-punch that Dan and I used when filing their papers in binders. Ellie, then seven, wanted to punch holes, Tye, age five, wanted to punch clothes, and Olivia, only two, just wanted. Invariably an argument arose. It became obvious that we needed to establish some rules. Dan and I set up taking turns and disallowed punching clothes and skin. We figured out a system to use the hole-punch rather than taking it away.

Managing a time like *Soul Sunday* helps by remembering five guidelines:

- Be loving
- Be prepared
- Be patient
- Be calm
- Be creative

If a problem arises, like confusion over an issue or a fight over a hole-punch, consider the following:

Soul Sunday
Ten Problem-Solving Suggestions

1. Acknowledge the problem
2. Address the concern
3. Ask how the issue is relevant to the lesson
4. Let everyone share their viewpoint

5. Understand their fears
6. Recognize internal struggles
7. Offer analogies and personal experiences
8. Work together
9. Empower kids to find answers on their own
10. Remind each other about faith

Sometimes a child's personal problem can become a teaching tool. For example, if a child is particularly small or being bullied, a solution can be found in the Playshop about David and Goliath in Part II of this book. We used this biblical account to learn about faith and bravery. After reading the story together and talking about particular themes, we helped the kids make large cardboard shields. Next, we covered old wrapping paper tubes in foil to make swords (a substitute for a slingshot). Finally, Dan became Goliath, and the kids had lots of fun attacking him. The project involved art, theater, and big fun. Playshops can fit your family's particular purpose and reinforce the issues that are relevant to your family.

Soul Sunday will open doors for everyone involved. Communication between siblings and parents grows stronger. *Soul Sunday* is an opportunity to develop relationships with each other. Engaging children in activities and conversation increases their faith, respect, intellect, and trust. *Soul Sunday* will enhance their self-esteem and confidence will grow. *Soul Sunday* will develop more love between siblings, parents, and a divine spirit. And, it is a time for fun!

TWO

Discover Spirituality

Teach this triple truth to all: A generous heart, kind speech, and a life of service and compassion are the things which renew humanity.
—The Buddha

When my youngest was a toddler we called her the stealth bomber. She'd sneak off somewhere without a sound and explode with disaster or laughter, sometimes both. Once we heard her on the baby monitor but could not find her. She laughed. We followed the sound. She giggled again. Finally, we found her under our bed, inside a suitcase enjoying her time tricking us.

At the age of one Olivia had managed to make us laugh and scratch our heads. Children do that. They expose our weaknesses. They make us cry, laugh, and scream; and they hold our hearts. At a young age they begin to teach us profound lessons. In return we give them an abundance of love. We build their confidence. We help them answer difficult questions. At least we try. We hope we make them feel safe and secure and instill in them an ethical and moral belief system based on love and faith. We hope this will help guide them through life, long after they have left our homes. But how do we do it? It is a question that begets more questions.

How do we discover spirituality? How do we build faith? How do we delve into philosophical questions that are almost impossible to grasp? What happens when we try? The very thought of being responsible for someone else's spiritual well being, let alone our own, is so daunting that many people abandon it altogether. We leave it up to others: to our churches, temples, sanctuaries, and schools. But children look to parents first for guidance. Parents have a unique opportunity to raise spiritual and moral children. Taking time to be involved and teaching children compassionate values and spiritual ethics will lead to a community of insightful, strong individuals.

Where do we begin? Parents start by making a commitment to enter into a special time, like *Soul Sunday*, to engage their children. Prioritize a time to coach children through contemplation to help them discover what matters in life. Some of the most important goals of *Soul Sunday* are:

Soul Sunday
Ten Components for a Meaningful Life

1. Love
2. Compassion
3. Integrity
4. Kindness
5. Wisdom
6. Purposeful Work
7. Peace
8. Citizenship
9. Appreciation
10. Faith

These values and actions work in harmony with each other to create profound relationships. They are essential to living well and with purpose. Without them, we live in a state of fear, anxiety, cruelty, and aggression. Because the development of relationships is key to spiritual growth, it is important to understand the people we surround ourselves with in our own lives. The heart of *Soul Sunday* is to learn how to develop meaningful relationships with God, with family, and with people different from ourselves.

One of the most important relationships in my life is with my parents. After my dad began to recover from life-threatening surgery, he had many hours to contemplate life in the ICU. It was a difficult time for us all, and I asked him what lessons he had taken from the experience. There were many. The first gift of advice my dad offered surprised and saddened me. He asked that we not pass by a hospital bed without stopping to talk to the patient. He knew that the patient was lonely and isolated.

Although my dad's suggestion was based on a personal experience, he did not say it with self-pity. He knew he was lucky. My mom was at his side when visiting hours allowed. He had an enormous number of friends sending prayers, cards, and phone calls. The kind of loneliness he felt was one filled with isolation. He was isolated in his thoughts because none of us had shared in the same experience.

It made me understand the importance of two things. First, I realized the crucial need for a spiritual connection and relationship with God. Fortunately, my dad had this. I'm sure he felt a bit forsaken while lying alone in a hospital bed at 2:00 a.m., but there was no question about his faith. However, what I realized next was the need to share experiences, especially important ones, with others.

I remember how important it was to retell my "labor" story with other moms after I gave birth. They asked questions and offered comments different from my husband's thoughts. It wasn't that he didn't try to understand, but moms, who had their own stories to tell, helped me in another way. They could relate to the experience.

Creating relationships with people who can share and understand similar experiences is important to help us move through difficult times. After my brother died from the HIV virus, I needed to connect with others, and I wanted to serve a purpose. To help ease my pain I volunteered as an educational speaker for an AIDS organization. Birth, death, and illness are important times for people to find support from others. Relationships serve many purposes, but all of them ultimately help us grow as individuals.

It is in relationship that we connect to others and the greater community. As our society continues to integrate diversity and learn about people with different experiences, cultures, and religions, it is important to reach out and make contact. Sharing our own experiences with others will help create mutual understanding and peace.

In a diverse country, making connections with others deepens and enriches our lives. Not all relationships are easy, but by teaching our children their importance, they learn to collaborate and live less lonely lives. In their book, *Developing Intercultural Awareness*, Robert Kohls and John Knight tell about a visitor from Sudan who made the following comment about culture in the United States:

> The hardest thing for me to accept and get used to when I first came to your country was how impersonal and inhuman everything was. Whenever I bought a Coca-Cola or chocolate bar or a postage stamp I had to buy it from a machine rather than from a living person. You can't talk to a machine, and even when it gives you a candy bar, a machine cannot give you a satisfying relationship. But in your country many people want to spend their time by themselves rather than by talking to other people in a friendly conversation.[3]

Culture in the United States moves at such a frenetic pace that Americans often neglect to develop meaningful relationships and miss a key part of life.

Hopefully we all have one friend, one family member, a spouse, or a partner who we would lie down and die for. Think about who that person is. If someone is lucky, she or he may have three or four such relationships. The characteristics that create such bonds can be taught during *Soul Sunday*.

By committing to a time like *Soul Sunday*, children will learn to communicate, collaborate, and develop confident convictions. As children develop spiritually, they build their relationship with God, a higher power, and with nature and each other. They learn that life is bigger than they are. Many children live in a sheltered world with their greatest concern being a baseball game, their algebra test, or the winner of TV's hottest reality show. Establishing a particular time for communication and creating a weekly or monthly ritual will develop relationships and ground family life. A ritual provides structure and develops a commitment from those involved. Although there are many reasons for a consistent time and space to do *Soul Sunday*, I have outlined ten:

Soul Sunday's
Ten Reasons for Ritual

1. To make faith a priority
2. To enhance communication
3. To recognize conflicts
4. To overcome problems
5. To increase self-esteem
6. To grow joyfully and wisely
7. To connect to other cultures
8. To explore safely and securely
9. To worship God and life
10. To establish relationship

Developing a forum for family discussion and reflection strengthens spirituality. Once a forum like *Soul Sunday* is established with goals and guidelines, families can begin to explore what it means to have faith. Faith is essential to discovering and developing spirituality.

Literary scholar and writer Fenton Johnson wrote in his book, *Keeping Faith*:

> Faith is first among the theological virtues because all virtue proceeds from it, including and especially love. Faith is the leap into the unknown, the entering into an action or a person knowing only that I will emerge changed, with no preconceptions of what that change will be. Its antonym is cynicism, born of fear. Prosperous America is a fear-filled society because we are a faithless society. Without faith, without that willingness to embrace life, including its uncertainty and pain and mortality and mystery, the soul becomes stagnant.[4]

Spirituality and faith are interlinked. We cannot physically see God or a higher power; however, we can accept that life is not just about us alone. Creating a space like *Soul Sunday* and having a podium to talk about spirituality help families define their personal beliefs.

Many of the books I've read throughout the years have contributed to my personal beliefs. I have joined a variety of book clubs to discuss different viewpoints. Invariably books are chosen that people both like and dislike. While attending one book club we discussed *Traveling Mercies* by Anne Lamott. The book itself is the retelling of a spiritual journey by the author. As a single mom she brings up many struggles related to parenting. My friends and I could relate to her tales of anxiety about making the right choices for our children.

That evening we found ourselves discussing our own dilemmas and spiritual journeys. With forty years of experience we had all confronted difficult issues and questioned our roles in life. We recognized that we were all on different paths. Many in the group, whether deeply religious or not, recognized their inhibitions about discussing faith. Some felt threatened by outsiders with deep convictions and expressed anger over their judgmental attitudes. Some in the group mentioned their embarrassment about a lack of religious knowledge, while others were not comfortable expressing their beliefs.

All of us had different opinions and convictions about religion and faith. Whether it was the "please, please, please" or "help me, help me, help me" prayers that come in times of trauma, or the "thank you, thank you, thank you" offerings, we found ourselves all connecting to sacred questions and concerns.

At some point in life we question the paths our lives have taken, the experiences that have occurred, and the blessings we have received. *Soul Sunday* is a way to begin a conversation about our different experiences. *Soul Sunday* is designed to help guide families in a spiritual quest, as well as to help children and adults better understand different religions in our growing pluralistic society. A family grows purposefully through healthy, respectful interactions. Establishing relationships by creating a time and space like *Soul Sunday* will develop spirituality and explore personal faith. Embark.

THREE

Faith, Fear, and Fretful Objections

Faith is the assurance of things hoped for, the conviction of things not seen.
—Hebrews 11:1

In the fall of 2005 my dad had a high-risk surgery that went awry. My sister called, unsure that he would survive the morning. I quickly made a reservation, packed, and kissed my family good-bye. As the early morning flight left Denver I ignored the man typing on his laptop next to me, pretended to sleep when orange juice was served, and silently offered many, many prayers. I landed in North Carolina hoping my dad was still alive.

After a series of surgeries, he stabilized long enough for me to fly back home and reassure my own kids that life was not falling apart. I didn't know exactly what to tell them. No one knew if Papa would survive. Life became both instantly vulnerable and fragile, but it was life. We held onto that.

Instead of waiting for Sunday to arrive, we held *Soul Sunday* on a Tuesday that week. We needed to be sad together. We needed to gather our prayers and all our energy to send Papa's way. The kids did not talk about death then. They talked about life. For this, I was grateful.

We drew cards to send to Papa. We sang him songs on tapes and told him stories. We sent my mom cards too. Ellie wrote a note on her card saying, "The sun will come out at some point." We talked about the Native American saying, "There are no rainbows without tears."

Holding a ritual like *Soul Sunday* helped relieve the anxiety for my family. Between us, we had communal worship, a time to share, and a time to reflect. We created the groundwork for communication and faith. Like deeply devout Christians or Buddhists who meditate daily, we understood how the ritual of prayer and meditation could carry a person through extreme struggles.

Crisis happens. People labor with misfortune, illness, divorce, loss, and pain throughout their lives. Finding a time for prayer or meditation connects people to a greater force. Reminding children of their relationship with a more powerful spirit helps them navigate through feelings of helplessness and fear.

What stops families from helping their children develop faith and respect for others with different beliefs? One answer is fear. Fear is an emotion we don't always recognize, but its effects are debilitating. Fear can paralyze people from moving forward. Without taking steps to learn about new and different ideas, people limit themselves.

Children's fears sometime seem simplistic. Big dogs, spiders, monsters, bullies, weird-looking food, and strangers are just a few of their many concerns. Some adults are afraid of the same things, and the list often accumulates as we get older. Instead of weird-looking food, adults grow to be afraid of weird-looking people. Strangers become terrorists. Spiders may actually stay spiders, but other fears get added to the list: financial concerns, war, illness, trauma, and so on.

Talking to our kids about their fears and how to gain comfort makes it easier to understand our own fears as well. Once during *Soul Sunday*, Dan and I shared the tale about Jonah. Jonah is a story found in the Hebrew Bible or Old Testament. God asks Jonah to do something, but Jonah doesn't listen. While sailing across the Mediterranean Sea, Jonah is tossed overboard and swallowed by a large fish. Jonah does not die. He rests inside the fish while God talks. This time, Jonah listens, is freed, and continues to live his life doing what God asks.

Our youngest was concerned about the story. She wanted to know why God made a fish swallow Jonah. She was afraid of that kind of a god. Dan and I explained that in this particular legend, God moved Jonah to a quiet place where he could hear God. Sitting inside a fish's mouth is a pretty good place for listening. Olivia understood, and her fear about a wrathful God subsided.

Talking about what we don't know or don't understand helps to ease insecurities rather than to create them. All three of our kids at some point in their development asked the same three questions:

- How can God see everything?
- How can God hear all of our prayers?
- How would they be noticed by God?

As parents, we don't have all the answers. Neither does one particular religion. None of us know exactly what is right and what will happen. We build our faith from our relationship with God. Faith often becomes framed by the institutions we join and the life that we live. Our spiritual quest becomes a question rooted in faith. We trust in what we do not know.

As parents, we can nurture the ability to trust in ourselves and in a divine power. It is important to realize that we don't always have command of our lives. We all like to control, some of us more than others. However, we can't always know, and we can't always control. Sometimes the sacrifice of power helps us develop our faith. As parents we can encourage our children to listen to their inner selves, to their hearts, and to God who is always with them.

Developing our spirituality will help ease fears. It is important for parents to help develop a sense of security however, it's also important to be honest. By giving false information or by altering answers to calm fears, rumors can begin and more fears develop. Being sincere with ourselves about what we are afraid of builds genuine communication. It is OK to let our kids know we don't always know the answers.

When studying the Bible, or any religious stories, kids will inevitably ask, "Is this true?" What they are really asking is, "Did this actually happen?"

Lutheran Pastor Rich Mayfield put it succinctly when he said:

Read the Bible uncritically, at least at first. Don't get caught up in whether this or that could actually happen…enter into it! Live the story first, and study it later. To get bogged down in whether this is fact or that is fiction is to run the risk of missing out on what is profoundly true.[5]

Studying a religion involves keeping an open mind. Having faith involves believing in the unknown, not in literal text. Religious philosopher and author Marcus Borg speaks at length in his books about the difference between literal and metaphorical thought.[6] There are ways to learn from the Bible, the Torah, or any religious text without accepting them as the absolute truth. It is possible to believe in the teachings of Jesus or of Moses without depending on the exact words of the texts that have been told, retold, and translated.

All religions have extreme fundamentalists who take everything literally. Most extremists believe they are right. Such righteousness is spawned from control and from fear. It is time to be honest with what we do not know to be exactly true, and have faith in the journey God has provided us. In their book *If God is Love*, Pastors Philip Gulley and James Mulholland say the following:

> A lack of curiosity demonstrates our fear and disrespect for others. An easy assurance in our righteousness and right thinking makes it nearly impossible for us to consider any new idea. We become truth keepers rather than truth seekers—quick to speak and slow to listen. This unwillingness to listen to those who think differently is not a sign of faithfulness, but an unwillingness to hear God's messengers…Gracious religion isn't an unbending allegiance to a narrow orthodoxy. It is about approaching our life with God and others in a spirit of gentleness, humility, and openness.[7]

During a *Soul Sunday* session we held near Easter time, Dan and I brought up the word *suffering*. What did it mean to the kids? They had heard the word before, but as with many words in the Bible or in other religious texts, we weren't sure if they knew what it meant.

Our eldest, Ellie, suggested the word meant that you get hurt. She gave an example about a friend who could hurt your feelings by not letting you play. Tye, age five at the time, said you could get hurt by a rock. He added that you might bonk your head on a tree, or maybe, even, that a bully would push you in a puddle and you would get angry. Olivia, not quite three, said that suffering might be when she feels mean, or when people are mean. These were very age-appropriate answers and very telling for us as parents.

Through our dialogue Dan and I understood our kids' worries and were able to ease their anxiety. We talked simply and yet pointedly about their feelings of fear, sadness, and suffering. We offered solutions and gave our own examples of apprehension.

After we addressed our own concerns, we talked about how we might contribute to the suffering of others. With very simple examples we discussed how we feel when we hurt others, even if it's an accident. It helped the kids to understand that God offers "do-overs." Finally, we talked about other people and their pain. Developing empathy is one step toward tolerance. It also helps children feel less alone when they are challenged with difficult feelings. We discussed emotions that are held by people all over the world, regardless of their religious preferences.

A heightened awareness of people who have similar emotions and feelings creates a common thread. It makes us less afraid of each other when we find similarities. If we teach our children to be accepting and help build their confidence rather than their fears and fretful objections, they will become more broadminded.

Educating children and creating an atmosphere of tolerance and acceptance is crucial to world peace. Eleanor Roosevelt talked often about this idea. She noted, "For it isn't enough to talk about peace. One must believe in it. And it isn't enough to believe in it. One must work at it." Creating a time for *Soul Sunday* will help instill faith, justice, communication, and an understanding about different cultures and religions. Letting go of our fears or at least recognizing them will lead to open, genuine dialogue. Our children deserve no less.

FOUR

Spinning the Religious Wheel

If we lose love and self-respect for each other, this is how we finally die. It is time for parents to teach young people early on that in diversity there is beauty and there is strength.
—Maya Angelou

How do we teach our children about diversity? How do we face our own prejudices and move beyond them? How do we learn about different religions without anxiety? It's not an easy task, but, in today's interdependent world, an essential mission.

To help our kids identify with other cultures and to help them understand why people value different kinds of faith, Dan and I have used many tools in our *Soul Sundays*. We've pulled out an atlas, spun the globe, traveled and met people, attended different religious services, and visited both inner cities and lands far away.

Studying about a religion is different from understanding a culture, in that it becomes an intimate process. Faith is personal for everyone. Learning about another religion involves respect, and appreciating a difference is not the same as converting to it. A family can solidify their own belief system while learning about others.

Dan and I introduced our children to global religious differences during *Soul*

Sunday. We started with a safe subject and a topic other than religion that the kids would understand about a culture. We began with geography.

We talked about how a culture and a religion are both influenced by geography. Temperatures and locations play a role in the types of foods people eat and the clothing they wear. Someone living in the desert would not wear a snowsuit. People wear turbans and veils on their heads in reverence to God, but also to help protect them from the hot sun and stinging desert sand. We gave silly examples, and the kids laughed as they made sense of it. We gave more illustrations, and they asked more questions. It became an interesting discussion. Finally, Dan and I steered the question to religion. Almost immediately, Tye said, "I know God loves people all around the world, but he loves the good ones more than the bad." Ellie piped up and added, "Well, I think he lets the good people at least live longer."

I scratched my head. My kids had offered comments that were biased and judgmental. I wondered if we were handling this correctly. I didn't want them to see the world as good or bad in such simple terms. I didn't want my kids believing that God played favorites.

Dan and I looked at each other and realized we had this moment to teach something profound. We asked them to think about how we might help bad people become good people. We offered examples and opinions that weren't entirely black and white. We tried to steer the conversation away from absolutes. We wanted them to think how they could make the world "gooder" through their own contributions. We talked about how we, as individuals, might help the world become a better place.

Finally, we rounded the corner back to world religions. We handed them each a plastic circle and asked them to pretend the circles were steering wheels. Next we let them race around the room driving their imaginary cars. Mayhem. One child ran around the couch, another circled the table, and the third made all kinds of wild beeping, screeching sounds. Olivia tried to outrun her brother and squealed when she did. Tye's antics and volume increased. Ellie laughed from her belly.

After a few minutes we asked them to drive their cars back to the starting gate. We took away the wheels and discussed what happened: they all went in different directions, but they all found their way back to the starting gate. We explained that God was like the starting gate. God gave people different wheels of faith to find their way back to divinity.

We went to the counter and drew cars and glued on pasta wheels to remember the day. As we did, Ellie offered a comment, "God helps us steer by keeping us company and helping us from getting lost." Tye piped up as well. "God comes into our head and hearts to help us steer," he said. Encouraged by their participation Dan I moved forward with their analogy.

As they were drawing road signs on their maps, we talked about the road signs that different religions use. In Christianity the most common symbol is the cross. In Judaism the reigning symbol is the Star of David. Both Buddhists and Hindus revere the lotus flower, while Muslims often use a crescent moon as a symbol. Symbols have meaning that we, as humans, attach to them. The symbols serve as road signs. Our kids added symbols to their projects, and we tacked them on their bulletin boards. I turned the activity into a Playshop which is outlined in Part II.

Faith is a deeply personal issue, but it is also a cultural one. People are framed by their environment and often adhere to different religions based on their location, culture, and environment. However, as the world has become more fluid, people of different faiths live near one another. In a codependent world countries are now reliant on each other for both social and economic means. Peace cannot exist without people recognizing global interdependence and making a commitment to communication.

I recently had the honor of seeing and listening to the Dalai Lama. Ellie, nine at the time, came too. She thought he seemed a lot like Yoda, which was meant as a compliment. With a great sense of humor, he spoke earnestly and sincerely about peace. He suggested that annihilation of an enemy does not and will not work in today's world. We rely even on our enemies in today's global economy. If both parties swallow their pride and come to the table, communication and collaboration can lead to a new way of resolution. It is important to understand both the differences and the commonalities between people and their beliefs when working toward peace.

Interdependence in our society needs to be addressed but not feared. Better understanding of another world religion does not lead to a dismantling of one's own faith. The opposite is often the case. When someone opens the door to learning, the more genuinely convinced that person may become to his or her own beliefs.

As I began the process of teaching *Soul Sunday* to my kids, I realized I needed to be better educated myself. Although I had studied world religions in college I decided I needed to go back to my own roots in Christianity. I joined a Bible study group where I learned the meaning behind the stories I had learned as a child, but had never really processed. As my ideas began to develop I left that particular church and attended another. I pored over books that helped give me new clarity to my faith.

Instead of a blue-eyed, long-haired Jesus that I had stared at in a picture frame during Sunday School, I learned Jesus was a Jewish mystic, a brilliant and kind divine man, a social rebel, and a great teacher. He didn't teach to the "good" Christians. He ventured into the feared parts of town where lepers and outcasts lived. He excluded no one. Jesus didn't have prejudicial beliefs. He taught love. He lived it. It was from this place I wanted to teach my kids—to live a loving, passionate life full of respect for others, not prejudice.

Communicating with people from all walks of life was an essential part of Jesus' ministry. Stepping outside of a church or a temple and embracing the community's diversity would be more similar to the teachings of Jesus than condemning or being afraid of someone. Getting to know our neighbors and even learning to love and respect different people follows Jesus' example.

Unfortunately many people choose to live in a sheltered world. Sitting on the same pew and refusing to experience anything outside of one's limited culture does not create a sense of safety for children. We live in a global society, and our kids will be exposed to new and different ideas throughout their lifetime. It is better to prepare our children for a world of cultural diversity than to hide them from reality. The glass house that is built to protect a child is ultimately shattered.

Soul Sunday can be a time to expose kids to other religions in a safe format. Parents have the opportunity to answer questions, as well as to educate themselves. Of the estimated 4,200 religions in the world, the five I focus on are:

- Christianity   2.1 billion followers
- Islam   1.3 billion
- Hinduism   900 million
- Buddhism   376 million
- Judaism   14 million[8]

These religions can serve as a starting gate for parents to explore alternative religions and cultures. By engaging in the Playshops at the end of the book, readers are given tools to explore traditions from lands around the world. Learning about other religions will enhance personal beliefs and develop a stronger sense of spirituality. Doing it with our families develops communication, relationships, and self-esteem. Invite the world into your home!

Hinduism

Regarded as the world's oldest religion, Hinduism has its roots in India, 4000 BCE. Hindus believe consciousness began before the universe existed and that spirituality is rooted in consciousness bound by truth and eternal love. Hindus do not read one particular holy book or follow a single founder. Instead, Hindus trust a religious philosophy based on many rich customs.

Hinduism remains the dominant faith in India and is now the world's third largest religion. Hindus believe that a person can experience God directly. The Hindu belief system transcends western ideas about religion by merging science, faith, philosophy, and physical wellness into a universal consciousness guided by a divine and tolerant love. They believe God is in everything, so all life should be highly respected.

Although Hinduism has evolved over years it still remains a way of life for millions of people. Followers of Hinduism believe in a supreme deity who is represented by many different gods and goddesses. Many Hindus regard their belief as a universal science bound by love rather than as a religion.

Followers of Hinduism believe the ultimate goal for humans should be to free themselves of samsara, or the never-ending cycle of continuing life. To do this Hindus follow four aims or doctrines in their lives.

1. Dharma: fulfill a purpose, do your duty with ethical practice
2. Artha: create prosperity, work hard
3. Kama: gratify the pleasurable parts of life, enjoy
4. Moksa: find freedom from the cycle of birth and death, live with God

For Hindus, this doctrine evolves over time through a process called reincarnation. They believe one's soul will migrate through time by taking different life forms. The deeds of one life continue for better or worse in the next lifetime. This is called karma. Eventually, one will escape the cycle and reach enlightenment. The word Hinduism is actually derived from a word meaning "to flow." Hindus believe in the eternal flow of energy, time, and life.

Hindus follow five Yamas, or commandments, that one should not do and five Niyamas that one should pursue throughout a lifetime.

Yamas	**Niyamas**
1. Do not hurt	1. Be clean
2. Do not lie	2. Be content
3. Do not steal	3. Be self-disciplined
4. Do not indulge in excess	4. Be studious
5. Do not be greedy	5. Move toward God, surrender

Many tales of these ethical doctrines are outlined as poems, songs, and adventures in Hindu texts. The most important are the *Vedas* and the *Upanishads*, although the *Bhagavad Gita* is one of the best-known poems of the *Mahabharata*. Hindu texts describe many gods and goddesses, but the three most important are Brahma, the creator; Vishnu, the preserver and protector; and Shiva, both the destroyer and the re-creator. These three deities are considered the Holy Trinity of Hinduism, referred to as the Trimurti: God in three forms.

Followers of Hinduism visit a temple or mandir and practice meditation and yoga, and perform pujas (prayer rites) to define their practice. Hindus believe there are many paths to God. Prayer, work, diet, and physical exercise are all ways to reach the Divine. Above all, Hindus believe that at the core of any practice or incarnation, love must be present.

Buddhism

Like Hinduism, Buddhism began in Asia. Like Christianity, Buddhism began with the teachings of one man. Buddhism has now become a religion with adherents around the world. It is not only considered a religion, but also a philosophical way of living and daily discipline.

In the sixth century BCE, a young prince, Siddhartha Gautama, was born in what is now Nepal. Legend has revealed that an important sage prophesied that Siddhartha would one day become a great spiritual leader. Unhappy with the news, his parents built a large wall around their palace to protect him from the world. Siddhartha lived in the palace until he had a wife and son. However, he began to question what the outside world was like, and chose to leave.

Dismayed by the great poverty and suffering that he witnessed, Siddhartha renounced his wealthy inheritance and began a meditation practice sitting under a Bodhi tree. He became the Buddha by awakening to his true nature. His practice merged the attention of body and mind until he reached enlightenment.

Buddhism is now the fourth largest religion in the world and is comprised of four major traditions: Zen, Theravada, Tibetan, and Mahayana. These practices differ in philosophy and doctrine and are largely defined by geography. However, their core, fundamental beliefs remain consistent.

Buddhists believe in three main groups of laws: The Four Noble Truths, The Eightfold Path, and The Five Precepts.

The process of human suffering is referred to as The Four Noble Truths.

1. Dukkha: people suffer
2. Samudaya: people desire, and cravings are the cause of suffering
3. Nirodha: let go of desire to end suffering

4. Eightfold Path: follow the path to end suffering and desire

The Eightfold Path is a process to free individuals from suffering. To do this one must use discipline and intention to create:

- Right understanding of the The Four Noble Truths
- Right aspirations and thought, intention
- Right speech
- Right conduct and action
- Right livelihood
- Right effort
- Right mindfulness
- Right concentration

Following The Eightfold Path will lead to Nirvana, or enlightenment. Buddhists, like Hindus, also believe freedom from suffering may take many lifetimes to achieve, a process called reincarnation.

The third law consists of the Five Precepts.

1. Do not kill or destroy life
2. Do not steal
3. Do not be unchaste
4. Do not lie
5. Do not use intoxicants

Buddhists maintain a meditation practice, visit a temple or monastery, and follow three principles in their life. The principle of reciprocity, known as the Golden Rule, is necessary for a righteous life. A second principle is that Buddhists must develop one's mind through meditation. This is called Samadhi. The final principle is to reach enlightenment by maintaining a pure mind.

The goal of a Buddhist practice is to end suffering and awaken to one's true nature.

Judaism

Judaism, Christianity, and Islam all share the same origins and are referred to as the Abrahamic religions. Judaism began in about 2000 BCE. Both Christianity and Islam have roots in Judaism, but have diverged with their own leaders and beliefs. Although Judaism has a smaller population than other major world religions, it is still influential in world affairs.

All Abrahamic religions are monotheistic, following one supreme God. Jews, Christians, and Muslims consider Abraham to be God's earliest patriarch, and Jews believe they are the children of Abraham. Their faith is based on the belief that Yahweh, the Hebrew name for God, is omnipotent, omniscient, and omnipresent. All Jewish law is derived from Yahweh and establishes the ways to serve God. Judaism concerns itself with this life and what the individual does while he or she lives on earth. The religion encourages people to concentrate on what one does more than what one says he or she believes.

Abraham first led his family out of what is now Iraq, to the Promised Land, Israel/Palestine. His family members later moved to Egypt, but their descendants were taken into captivity as slaves. In about 1250 BCE, Moses led the Israelite people out of slavery, receiving the law at Mt. Sinai. This revelation became known as the Law of Moses, which consists of the first five books of the Hebrew Scriptures, referred to as the Old Testament. These books are known as the Torah.

Not only does the Torah outline the early history of the Jewish people, but it details God's law. The Ten Commandments were revealed to Moses by God.

1. I am the Lord thy God, and you shall have no other God before me
2. I am the only God, worship no idols
3. You shall not take the Lord's name in vain

4. Keep the Sabbath holy
5. Honor thy father and mother
6. You shall not kill
7. You shall not commit adultery
8. You shall not steal
9. You shall not lie
10. You shall not covet thy neighbors' goods

Considered sacred, the Torah is hand scribed in sections which are sewn together as a scroll. The scroll is wrapped in a mantle, and contained in an Ark of the Covenant. The Ark is kept inside a synagogue, where the Jewish congregation meets. The entire Torah is read over one year's time. In Orthodox Judaism, only men are allowed to study the Torah. At age thirteen Jewish children take part in a ceremony known as a bar/bat mitzvah, meaning that they then assume the religious responsibilities of Jewish adults.

The Jewish day begins at sundown. Jews consider both Friday night and Saturday until sundown the Sabbath day. On Friday night they host a Shabbat dinner to celebrate the day of rest, God, life, and creation. The Jewish New Year is celebrated in fall beginning with Rosh Hashanah and ending ten days later with Yom Kippur, the Day of Atonement. Repentance and doing good deeds are important virtues to the Jewish people. Family, community service, work, charity, and prayer are vital parts of Jewish life.

Oppressed over centuries, many Jews continued to lobby, politically, for their own country after the horrors of the Holocaust. The Zionist movement began in the mid-1800's and gained political momentum with Theodor Herzl's piece, *The Jewish State*. In 1948 the state of Israel was established.

Christianity

Christianity differs from all other world religions in that it claims Jesus lived here on earth as the divine son of God. Monotheistic in belief, Christians worship both God as the Supreme Being and Jesus, as his son.

Like most religions, there are many diverse groups of people who believe in Christianity. Although different churches and followers practice their faith in different ways, the basic theology of Christianity centers on Jesus Christ.

Christianity began in Israel/Palestine and spread throughout Greece and the Mediterranean world in the first century. Today it has become the world's largest religious faith.

As biblical stories contend, the angel Gabriel proclaimed the birth of Jesus, and Mary gave birth to Jesus in Bethlehem. Jesus was born into a Jewish family, and at about the age of thirty, began his ministry. He chose twelve disciples to follow him throughout Palestine preaching the Golden Rule: do unto others as you would have them do unto you. Jesus was a Jewish mystic and social activist who disagreed with much of the social and religious practice of the time. Through parables, healing, and teaching, Jesus taught nonviolence, love, and forgiveness.

The biblical accounts differ regarding the length of Jesus' ministry, but most scholars argue that it lasted between one and three years. Jesus was sentenced to death by leaders of the Roman Empire and was crucified on a cross. His first followers, who would come to be known as Christians, and those to follow believe that he rose from the dead on the third day. Jesus interacted with his followers for forty days after his resurrection and then ascended to heaven. Many Christians believe humans are born sinful, but by believing in Jesus Christ, they can be saved and brought to God.

Christians believe that God exists simultaneously as the Father, the Son, and the Holy Spirit, referred to as the Holy Trinity. Following Jewish tradition, Christians believe in the law of the Old Testament. Although Jesus never wrote about his belief or faith in God, many of his followers did. Jesus' disciples, led by Peter, spread the story and teachings of Jesus throughout the Mediterranean world.

The New Testament was created by Jesus' followers after Jesus died. The first four books, written by Matthew, Mark, Luke, and John, are considered the gospel, which means "Good News" in Greek. Much of the rest of the New Testament was written by Paul, a Jewish convert, who wrote letters to large communities, urging them to believe in Christianity as a way of life.

The church was established as an institution for communities to learn about Christ. Christianity has great diversity amongst its followers. Some churches maintain doctrines that are orthodox while others are less rigid in their interpretation of the Bible.

According to www.adherents.com the largest denominational families in the United States are:

2004 Estimated Population

Catholic	71,796,719
Baptist	47,744,049
Methodist/Wesleyan	19,969,799
Lutheran	13,520,189
Presbyterian	7,897,597

Islam

Followers of Islam are Muslims, who believe in one God. They believe Moses, Jesus, Abraham, and other central biblical figures were prophets sent from God. Muslims deem the last prophet sent by Allah (the Arabic name for God) was Muhammad, born in about 575 CE, and that his teachings are God's final revelation.

At the age of forty Muhammad began his lessons in Mecca and was sent a revelation by the angel Jibril (Gabriel in English). It was Jibril who revealed the Qur'an, the Islamic holy book, to Muhammad. The Qur'an is considered the true and final word of God for all Muslims. The *Hadith* is an important text for Muslims that gives more quotes and explanations by Muhammad.

After his revelation, Muhammad tried to convert many of the pagan countrymen but was met by great resistance. He moved farther north to Medina on a trek called the Hijira. The hajj, or pilgrimage, became a turning point for Muhammad. He developed a following and returned to Mecca as a renowned guide. Muhammad became a powerful leader in Arabia and established Islam throughout the region.

The word Islam is a derivation from Salam, meaning peace. Islam can also be translated as a surrendering or submission. All Muslims are to submit their life to God. They believe Islam should rule over one's life as well as the community.

Islam maintains Five Pillars of Faith, which serve as behavioral guidelines.

1. Shahadah or faith: believe that there is no god but Allah, and Muhammad is his Prophet
2. Salat or Prayer: pray five times a day in the direction of Mecca
3. Zakat or Charity: give offerings to the poor
4. Sawm or Fast: fast during daylight hours throughout the holy month of Ramadan

5. Hajj or Pilgrimage: every Muslim (specifically male) who is able should journey to Mecca

In addition to the Pillars of Faith, Muslims believe people should not gamble, drink, eat pork, lie, be sexually promiscuous, or steal. Defiance of these moral convictions may result in severe penalty. Muslims believe there is a Day of Judgment and that one's soul will be delivered to either heaven or hell, depending on one's behavior and faith.

Muslims pray five times a day by kneeling on a prayer mat facing the holy city of Mecca. Many pray at a mosque, which is the central place of worship and life of a Muslim community. The rules of the Qur'an govern not only the individual but the entire community. Although it is the youngest of the major world faiths, Islam is projected to become the largest religion by the end of the twenty-first century. It is currently followed by believers all over the world but predominantly in the Middle East, Southeast Asia, and Africa. Although many people think most Muslims are Arabs, only about twelve percent of Muslims worldwide are Arabs.[9]

FIVE

Connecting Culture and Community

"What is REAL?" asked the Rabbit one day. "Does it happen all at once, or bit by bit?" "It doesn't happen all at once," said the Skin Horse. "You become. It takes a long time. That's why it doesn't often happen to people who break easily, or have sharp edges, or who have to be carefully kept. Generally, by the time you are Real, most of your hair has been loved off, and your eyes drop out and you get loose in the joints and shabby. But these things don't matter at all, because once you are Real you can't be ugly, except to people who don't understand.
—*The Velveteen Rabbit*, Margery Williams

During a *Soul Sunday* a few years ago, my family was sitting on the floor next to a large glass window and talking about friendship. Not all our sessions are religious in the literal sense. Some center around values, ethics, and important lessons life has to offer. Olivia, two at the time, was getting bored with the details of fickle and fastidious friendships that Tye and Ellie were trying to understand. She rolled over on her back, looked up, and asked, "Why does God come to our house? Does he like snow?"

Given that the question was asked in May and it was indeed snowing outside, it made sense. While Tye and Ellie were trying to configure the makings of friendship on the playground, Olivia was thinking about how and why God might be a friend. For her, living at ten thousand feet in the Colorado Rockies meant that snow came more often than not. She was trying to make a connection out of snow, God, and friendship. To her, friendship meant someone coming to the house to play…even in the snow.

For all of us, I believe, it is important to not only understand how and why God is important to us, but to realize how and why God is important to others. A healthy curiosity is far better than living in fear. Learning about a different religion does not require conversion. It does, however, encourage tolerance. We may not always agree or even respect people with different values from our own, but in this global society, it is essential to understand them.

The world is not the same as it was one hundred years ago. Farmers from the American Midwest, like my grandparents, remind us of the major differences to-day's youth are confronted with. Among other things, we have an international community. After World War II, the Cold War, 9/11, and Iraq, it should come as no surprise that what happens in one country, will affect another.

When helping children understand our interdependence in the world, it is best to begin simply. Studying a common theme or subject that many cultures recognize will help kids make connections to the world at large. Children respond best with positive reinforcement, so beginning with likenesses, rather than differences, will have more impact on their learning. Once they have a sense of empathy and understanding, parents can move into more difficult subjects of discrimination and prejudice.

One example of a common theme is the harvest season. Societies across the world celebrate the harvest by calling it Thanksgiving, Sukkoth, and Moon Festival, to name only a few. Engaging kids in a *Soul Sunday* session about the harvest can take many forms. Families can plant a few seeds outside, shop at a fruit stand, or visit a farm. Many Americans have a background in farming. This is a great way to identify with oneself and then with another culture that harvests crops. There are a few examples in the Playshops at the end of this book.

Growing up in the Midwest has given me an understanding of family farming in Ohio and Indiana. Until I made a few road trips with college friends in Colorado, I thought all families in this country spent hours counting silos while on road trips in Chrysler station wagons.

My family, like most families, no longer farms for a living. However, after my parents retired they doubled the size of their garden. Once, they sent our kids a zucchini the size of a baseball bat. When they visit my parents, Ellie, Tye, and Olivia help pick peas, plant seeds, dig for worms…and learn a little about natural resources as well.

Any connection children can make with nature is a great way to identify with other cultures. If no one in the family has a garden, help the kids plant a bean seed in a paper cup. Realizing the seed needs water, sunshine, and a little TLC will help them relate to how and why a harvest celebration carries such meaning. From here, the discussion can move to other cultures and how they honor nature.

Nature studies can involve animals, which is another great theme for kids. Recently I went to a church service, and the pastor focused his sermon on animals. He explained that St. Francis, the patron saint of animals, dedicated his life to extending kindness to others, including animals. He gave great accounts of animal stories and spoke to us about caring, loving, and honoring all of God's creations, animals and plants included.

Many cultures connect to animals. Some Native Americans identify with a "power animal" and have elaborate ceremonies naming a child after an animal. For

Soul Sunday, Dan and I talked about animals and nature, and then asked our kids to connect to a power animal.

Ellie, who often has difficulty choosing, picked three. Because she loves dolphins, she associated herself with them as swimmers, and smart, playful, kind animals. She also chose an ant, she said, because they are hard to notice, but are strong and hard working. Finally, she chose an eagle, soaring in the sky.

Tye chose a shark because a shark is king of the sea. They love to eat and to swim, they are fierce, and can be slippery and soft. Olivia, at age three, didn't even have to think about it. She piped up and said she'd chosen a mouse because they are small, cute, quiet, and yet very sneaky. The children surprised us with their insightful choices. They drew pictures of their animals, and we added them to their *Soul Sunday* folders. The process helped them connect with nature and animals, and it helped them define their own qualities. It also helped them realize how unique we all can be and how everyone has been given special gifts…humans and non-humans alike.

Animals can be a terrific way to reach kids. They can be less complicated and easy to identify. Different religions honor animals in many ways. Hindus offer the highest regard for animals. Cows are considered sacred, and they can be seen walking across streets in the villages of India. Most Hindus are vegetarian and have a profound sense of respect for all living creatures. This is a beautiful aspect of Hinduism that children can identify with at an early age. Learning about another culture helps us understand how the religion has an impact on daily life .

Religion is just one aspect of culture, but it is an important one. Culture also encompasses history, geography, economics, as well as the more superficial attributes like food, dress, clothing, and other characteristics that an elementary school's "world day" might highlight. Looking at all aspects of a group of people goes beyond learning about tacos and turbans.

Understanding a broader picture of a culture not only enriches life, but contributes to breaking down cultural barriers, prejudice, and misunderstandings. According to Webster's dictionary, culture is defined "by the act of developing the intellect as the pattern of human behavior depending on one's capacity for learning and transmitting knowledge to succeeding generations." Believe it or not, Webster's uses a lot more words to describe culture, but for our purpose here, let's refer to culture as life.

In the anthropological sense, culture is how a group of people defines their actions based on their belief system. The way people dress, eat, and act; the kind of music they listen to or the art they appreciate; the buildings and schools they build…all are based upon a deeper meaning. A culture has its roots in the geography, politics, history, and religion of its people. For example, a person in Japan might eat sushi because fresh fish are abundant. Japan is a country made up of many islands and its geography affects the cuisine.

Another example I share with kids involves Halloween. Imagine someone who knows nothing about the USA, entering a school or a neighborhood on October 31. Would they think Americans' diet consists of candy and caramel apples? Would they think Americans dress oddly? Would they think we all worship a pumpkin? Learning about a culture involves discovering more than clothing and foods. It involves understanding something about the economics, history, geography, and religion of a group of people.

Religion is one essential component to understanding a culture. It will help explain why someone might celebrate a different holiday or why a person might wear a complicated piece of clothing. By failing to understand the religious background of a person, incorrect assumptions can be made that lead to harmful stereotypes and prejudicial behavior. The deeper meaning and background of a culture is pivotal to creating a more peaceful world.

I encourage parents and grandparents to explain, when they are engaged in a *Soul Sunday* lesson, the basics of each religion, as well as to explore history, geography, and even the politics of a country or culture. Obviously, this needs to be handled in an age-appropriate way. I have outlined activities in the Playshop section by ages, but remaining flexible is important. For example, while younger children are coloring and gluing, a parent might spend time researching history with an older child. One parent might talk to a child about a political issue while the other helps a child complete a project. There are many ways to diversify the activity.

Learning about the deeper aspects of a culture can be rewarding. Children will make connections to their lifestyles when comparing the differences between cultures. Communities can appear different by their clothing, food, habits, and language, but appreciating groups of people must go beyond superficial differences. Understanding the history, geography, politics, and religion of a group of people helps us truly appreciate a culture. *Soul Sunday* is designed to be time for families and to connect with others cross-culturally.

SIX

Soul Sunday's Logistics and Learning

God enters by a private door into every individual.
—Ralph Waldo Emerson

Last night we conducted *Soul Sunday* during the Jewish Rosh Hashanah holiday dinner. It's good to integrate variety into *Soul Sunday*, and this dinner proved to be no exception. As an alternative to sitting on the floor, we moved our venue to the dining room table and talked while enjoying a feast.

Dan led *Soul Sunday* by giving a brief introduction to the Jewish holiday. He explained that the Jewish New Year is a ten-day reflection and celebration, beginning with Rosh Hashanah and ending with Yom Kippur, the Day of Atonement. During that period Jews spend time in contemplation, thinking about events that occurred during the previous year and how they could improve life and themselves in the coming year.

To represent a sweet new year, families eat apples dipped in honey. Dan prepared the meal and offered us golden apple slices. While we ate crisp fruit dipped in syrupy clover honey we each reflected on our strengths and shortcomings. One by one we made suggestions about how we could improve our thoughts and behavior in the following year.

Dan began. He suggested that he try not to lose his temper so quickly during the kids' bedtime routine. Without missing a beat Tye turned his head toward me, pointed his finger, and said, "You need to do that one too, Mommy, except you're the owner of the mean voice in the morning time!" Out of the mouths of babes we realize our weaknesses.

As parents, all of us have things we say that we regret later. We wish we had been able to have a bit more patience. We wonder if what we've said, or yelled, will throw our kids into years of therapy. We do the best that we can and wonder if it will ever be enough.

The time shared together during *Soul Sunday* is not only an opportunity to be together and develop spirituality, it can be a time to re-evaluate relationships and how we communicate. When our kids remind us of our weaknesses, it is humbling. *Soul Sunday* can serve as a time to bow our heads, ask for guidance, and become stronger, better parents for it.

Both children and adults are confronted daily with situations that cause us to question who we are and what we believe in. *Soul Sunday* is an opportunity to change behaviors and to request both grace and guidance. As parents we can set positive examples that will help kids move through the hard times more quickly and easily, while at the same time admitting when we are wrong. Knowing that parents can make errors and 'fess up to them will help children do the same. Owning our mistakes will help us ultimately become more self-confident.

When we can be honest about our own insecurities and poor behaviors, our kids see us as human. They see us being humble. They see us not as invincible, but rather, as vulnerable. Knowing that parents will make mistakes can help kids understand their own mishaps, apologize, and recognize humanity's imperfections.

From this self-effacing place, human beings can grow. We can grow as individuals, and we can grow as a society.

While being honest, it is humbling sometimes to realize we are all human, and all make mistakes. This is important for kids to understand. They may feel a heightened need for perfection if their role models cannot apologize or recognize their own shortcomings. *Soul Sunday* is a good time to recognize our faults.

One Sunday in late May, eight and a half year old Ellie offered an announcement, reminding us all of our shortcomings. The school's year-end deadlines that often overrun parents were taking a toll on Dan and me. Days were filled with field trips, recitals, banquets, and year-end parties, while students, parents, and teachers raced toward the finish line. While feeling the strain of all these obligations I hadn't realized my oldest felt the pressure as well.

Ellie asked us all to convene in the living room. She would not begin until all were present and sitting. She declared that she was not happy with the current state of affairs and had something to say to all of us. She took one look at me and said I was expecting too much of her the last few weeks of school. She told Tye he was bothering her too much. Ellie looked Olivia directly in the eye and told her a sister did not need to be so bossy. Finally, she told Dan that he had not been fair in solving arguments. She adjourned her formal meeting by telling us all she was headed out to play, alone.

Such confident communication does not come without having a sense of high self-esteem and a certain comfort zone. I credit *Soul Sunday* with the ability to challenge us all. As parents, we were tremendously proud of Ellie that day. Dan and I assured her we would work on our behavior and thanked her for sharing. A few weeks later she told us all we had definitely improved. Phew.

Taking time for spirituality directly improves confidence, communication, and self-awareness. Outlined below are steps to help set up a *Soul Sunday* practice.

Soul Sunday
Steps to Creating a Setting

- Set a day for Soul Sunday (We chose Sunday because it was the one night we usually had few commitments and could really relax. Another family may choose to do a Soul Saturday)
- Decide on a consistent time
- Create a relaxing and yet enticing environment
- Use pillows
- Go to a room you don't use often
- Use a room in a different context…like the kitchen floor!
- Light candles
- Replace a typical light bulb with a colored one for the evening
- Play international or ethnic music (see appendix for suggestions)

Soul Sunday
Steps to Developing Engaging Activities

- Begin with a song
- Give thanks with a simple prayer
- Find ways to include each family member
- Use one of the *Playshops* in Part II or prepare your own
- Do a project or activity
- Close with a song, prayer, or group family hug and high five

Keep it simple yet structured; fun yet meaningful. *Soul Sunday* will become a place to develop a stronger family bond and increase everyone's level of spiritual faith, and also become an environment to be both serious and silly.

Dan and I use *Soul Sunday* as a time to learn about the Judeo-Christian traditions and study other religious faiths. We also apply the time to talk about morals and ethics. On one Sunday, we chose money as the theme. We began by asking the kids if they knew where the Bible mentioned money. They gave a few examples, and then we asked if they knew when or why people needed money. Their answers involved the usual themes: food, shelter, and clothing, plus a few personal items on their list like a bike, a transformer, and, for our youngest, more chocolate. We asked if people could ever have too much money. We asked them if someone really needed five houses and one hundred pairs of shoes. They laughed at that example until they realized we were serious. Their eyes opened wider.

Our questions led to a discussion about greed, jealousy, and selfishness, and whether or not money can make you happy. Like most things, it came back to a healthy balance in life. We tried to impress upon the kids that money should be used for necessities, for some pleasure, and also for charity. All world religions make clear that charity is essential. In his book *Oneness*, Jeffrey Moses outlines the common attributes amongst different religions. He explains that the different faiths have the following to say about charity:[10]

Bounteous is he who gives to the beggar who comes to him in want of food and feeble.   *-Hinduism*

As a full jar overflowing pours out the liquid and keeps back nothing, even so shall your charity be without reserve—as a jar overturned.   *-Buddhism*

He that hath pity upon the poor lendeth unto the Lord; and that which he hath given will He pay him again.   *-Judaism*

Above all things have fervent charity among yourselves for charity shall cover the multitude of sins.   *-Christianity*

The Prophet said: "Give in charity and do not withhold it, otherwise Allah will withhold it back from you."   *-Islam*

It is important for kids to understand financial responsibility as well as the need to give back to society. Giving with a full heart connects us to a more universal relationship. All kinds of skills and fun activities can be used during a money session. The kids can count and sort, look up foreign currency in books or on the Internet, match dollars, talk about inflation and percentages, and continue to think about ways they can earn, save, spend, and give back.

After the Tsunami washed over Southeast Asia in 2004 we held a *Soul Sunday* that focused on natural disasters. We talked about the importance of helping others in need. We tried to help the kids understand their connection to a global tragedy. We continued to discuss the questions we can't answer…like why storms happen. I do not believe God's wrath causes raging wind. I believe it's simply the weather. However, paying attention to the weather, to nature, to our role in the environment, and to the suffering of people during catastrophe is important. At a young age our kids began to piece together a link between us and everything and everyone else. All three kids were under ten, but they grasped the concepts because we kept it simple.

Simplicity is often overlooked in today's culture. Dress up and play dough take a second seat to Game Boy and PlayStation. However, all kids love to pretend. Some computer games do take one's mind to make-believe lands, but imagination really finds itself in theatrical play. One warm summer evening we decided to move *Soul Sunday* outside, and we played charades. For our youngest two, who could not read at the time, we drew pictures for them to act out. The game became so entertaining, that the kids began doing mini-skits on their own.

Acting and pretending that we are someone else helps us realize what we can become. We talked about how we express ourselves, and how non-verbal communication plays a role in our ability to develop relationships. We discussed how we might want to change but aren't sure how. We talked about goals and dreams and believing in ourselves. Playing charades was also just great fun as a family. Not only was it something you think about doing but never do, it also was a time to help teach some valuable lessons.

One of the aspects of *Soul Sunday* that I like best as a parent is learning more about my kids. Of course, it is a time to study our faith, to teach children well, and to create strong bonds. However, it is also a valuable time to gain insight to the problems and issues they may have outside of the home. For example, by watching Tye during *Soul Sunday*, we learned that he communicated with passionate expression. He was the kid who jumped up, waved wildly, and chanted, "Ooh, ooh." We set the stage for *Soul Sunday* rather seriously and raising hands was part of the program. While Tye acted as if he were sitting on hot coals, Ellie followed along patiently, and Olivia refused to raise her hand: she kicked her foot up instead. We saw their personalities emerge in even the smallest of details.

Soul Sunday can also be a time to nurture behaviors and to slowly think about changing them. It can be a time to work on manners, respect, and admiration for each other's differences.

Once children recognize their own uniqueness, even within the context of the same family, they can begin to recognize that everyone has something special to offer. This is an important step toward acceptance rather than prejudice and injustice. Dr. Martin Luther King wrote the following in a letter from the Birmingham City Jail: "Injustice anywhere is a threat to justice everywhere. We are caught in an inescapable network of mutuality, tied in a single garment of destiny. Whatever affects one directly, affects all indirectly."[11] We all are interconnected.

When learning about other cultures and religions it is important to encourage kids to recognize peace and justice issues as well as similarities and differences between people. If we begin to see cultures differently, rather than as right or wrong, a more peaceful existence will develop between us. Rabbi Michael Lerner expounded on the importance of acceptance in his book, *The Left Hand of God*:

> Though I personally believe that a deeper truth is self-evident—namely, that all human beings deserve to be respected and their opportunities to develop their capacities for love, generosity, creativity, beauty, freedom, knowledge, expanding consciousness, solidarity with others, and connection to spirit given as much support as possible—I don't think there is anything self-evident about how to apply such a principle in any given historical situation. And so I remain very cautious about those who think there is one and only one right way to apply this or any other ethical or spiritual intuition.[12]

Creating a time and place to develop spirituality will help children become more tolerant and respectful of others. Keep an open mind and an open heart as you teach your children. As you begin to think about how to incorporate *Soul Sunday* into your lives, look over the appendix and suggested readings. Part II gives you guidance through a curriculum, but by no means do you need to follow it exactly. Do what is best for your family. Find creativity and communication while exploring spirituality. Make *Soul Sunday* a time to connect, reflect, learn, and laugh. Enjoy your time with your family!

Soul Sunday®

Part II

Soul Sunday
Playshops

Section One: Fall

Section Two: Winter

Section Three: Spring

Section Four: Summer

Soul Sunday Playshops

The Playshops in Part II are designed to guide and to reinforce a *Soul Sunday* session with kids. The Playshops give parents ideas to set up *Soul Sunday* lessons, and the hands-on activities reinforce meanings and themes. Children's memories improve if work and play involve practical application and tangible activities. During the Playshops important questions may arise. It is a terrific family time to have fun together while safely learning about diverse faiths.

The Playshops are set up by season, but parents may choose to step out of order and/or do just the Playshops that most interest the family. The Playshops begin with the fall season because children often associate calendars with new beginnings at school. Most Playshops take between 45 minutes to one hour and are designed for kids three through sixteen. However, younger children can still participate and older teenagers make great assistants.

A country or a religion is highlighted with each Playshop, and materials are listed. Each Playshop purpose outlines themes but again, parents may choose their own concentration. Parents and children can add to the Playshops by doing research on the Internet or in books. An extensive list of resources is included at the end of *Soul Sunday*.

Each Playshop works best with a little structure. It is important to have an opening and closing for every lesson. Prayers, songs, or blessings are all good ways to begin or to offer closure. Children feel safest and most secure with a predictable beginning and ending.

A lesson is offered for each Playshop and each project is described, so that parents can easily reinforce their points. Whenever projects and activities are done there should be supervision, and safety rules should be outlined. Some projects involve art, others take the family outside, and some send kids to the kitchen. Playshops are opportunities for learning and having fun together, not to have perfect projects.

Soul Sunday is intended to be a time for families to explore their own faith, to better understand others, and to create an environment of acceptance and tolerance for all realms of diversity. This is done while families explore and have fun together, the surest way to develop self-esteem and security for children. Create a wonderful journey!

Fall

Section One: Fall

Apples and Honey: Sweet and Sorry

Jewish New Year

Season:	Fall
Time:	45 minutes-1 hour
Country/Religion:	Judaism
Age:	2-14
Materials:	apples
	honey
	knife
	plate
	paper/pen

Theme: Atonement and forgiveness
Prayer
Jewish New Year
Goals

Opening: Blessing/Song/Prayer

Lesson:

Rosh Hashanah begins the Jewish New Year and literally means "head of the year." Families and friends gather for dinner after attending a religious service at a temple. During the service a ram's horn, called a shofar, is blown to signify the beginning of the year. Ten days later Jews complete the celebration by honoring Yom Kippur, the Day of Atonement. During the time between, Jews pray, repent, and reflect. This is the holiest part of the year for Jewish believers.

The Jewish New Year occurs in the fall, but the Hebrew calendar pre-dates our current calendar. In 2006, Jews celebrated the year 5767.

After talking about Rosh Hashanah and Yom Kippur with your children, compare and discuss your own traditions to welcome in a new year. Jews celebrate the New Year by remembering, reflecting, and asking God for a fresh beginning in the coming year. Explain what atonement and forgiveness means. Talk about why it is important for people to apologize, to forgive someone, and to create better goals in a new year. As a family you may want to create goals together as well as individually.

Project: Food Fun

Cut some apples into slices. Let your children drizzle them with honey. For each apple slice they eat, or for each seed you find, ask your kids to tell you something they are sorry for, something they can do better, and a goal they have for the coming year. While they are busy munching on apple slices and honey, write down their answers so you can keep them in *Soul Sunday* folders, on the refrigerator, or pinned a bulletin board.

Closing: Blessing/Song/Prayer

Lovely Lunar Lanterns

Tet Trung Thu: Vietnamese New Year

Season: Fall
Time: 45 minutes-1 hour
Country/Religion: Vietnam
Age: 4-14

Materials: white paper
                     construction paper
                     scissors
                     tape
                     markers/crayons
                     sequins/glitter
                     flashlight
                     yarn

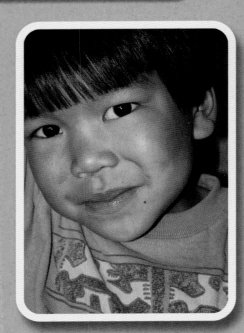

Theme: Remembrance
Prayer and ritual
Moon cycles and harvest celebrations
Vietnamese culture

Opening: Blessing/Song/Prayer

Lesson:

Many traditional cultures refer to the fall moon as the harvest moon. In Vietnam, an entire festival called Tet Trung Thu is devoted to the eighth lunar month. On the 15th day of the 8th month, people gather with lanterns to honor the full, bright glow of the moon. People feast on moon cake treats and parade through the streets with lanterns, which represent the moon's special glow.

During the festival of Tet Trung Thu people remember their loved ones who have died. They light incense and burn pretend paper money so that good wishes can be sent through the smoke to relatives who have passed away.

Originally, this celebration began just after harvest time in Vietnam. During the height of a busy harvest season, parents did not have much time to spend with their children. By mid-autumn, the harvesting was nearly complete, and Trung Thu became a celebration of both the abundant crops and of family togetherness. Much attention is devoted to children this festive time of year.

Spin the globe to find Vietnam. Open a discussion about farming, harvest, celebrating nature, moon cycles, thanksgiving and remembrance. Ask children to compare the Vietnamese celebration with their own traditions with similar themes.

Project: Paper Lanterns

Cut a rectangular piece of colored construction paper and place it lengthwise in front of you. Cut out shapes: diamonds, circles, hearts, etc., from the center of the paper. Kids can add glitter, paint, or sequins around their shaped holes to make it more elaborate. Tape the ends of the rectangle together to create a cylinder. Use a hole punch to make two holes at the top…one across from the other. Tie one end of a long piece (20 inches) of yarn in one hole and the other end of the yarn in the hole across from it. This will be the lantern's hanger. Take the lantern into a closet and let the kids hold a flashlight in it to light up their designs.

Closing: Blessing/Song/Prayer

Wheeling Religions

Introduction to world religions

Season:	Fall
Time:	45 minutes-1 hour
Country/Religion:	Global
Age:	2-11
Materials:	globe or map
	glue
	markers/paint
	uncooked pasta (wheels)
	paper plates

Theme: Introduce five major world religions:
   Hinduism, Buddhism, Judaism, Christianity, Islam
   Tolerance
   Respect
   Geography

Opening: Blessing/Song/Prayer

Lesson:

Introduce children to five major world religions—Hinduism, Buddhism, Judaism, Christianity, and Islam—through an activity. Give each child a paper plate and ask them to pretend it's a steering wheel. Tell the kids they have two minutes to race around the house. Ask them to find their way back to the starting gate when you blow a whistle. You can make the starting gate the kitchen table, a set of stairs, or any central location. On your mark, get set, go!

Once the kids have gathered back at the starting gate ask them if they all went the same direction. Notice if sound effects were used and if they came up against any roadblocks. This activity is an analogy used to describe the different religious paths people take. The start and finish gate is a metaphor for God. Families raise children in a particular culture, and find different roads to God. Each road is like a different religion. Emphasize that people take different paths, but none is right or wrong. Embellish the analogy and explain that symbols used by religions are like road signs along the way. Use a globe to show your kids where major religions are practiced and celebrated.

Project: Wheel Pies

This Playshop is unique in that it really has two projects. Use their paper wheels and draw four lines across the plate, which divides it into eight pieces. In each piece of pie write the name of a world religion. Use the empty slices for "other" religions not covered in this book.

Let kids color or paint uncooked pasta noodles shaped as wheels, and then glue them on to decorate the pie graph. Remind them that the wheels represent the different ways people believe in God.

Closing: Blessing/Song/Prayer

Dancing Diwali

Hinduism: Happy New Year

Season: Fall
Time: 45 minutes-1 hour
Country/Religion: India, Hinduism
Age: 2-14

Materials: tissue paper pieces
                     baby food jars
                     glue
                     small candles

Theme: Hinduism
Indian culture
Renewal
Illumination

Opening: Blessing/Song/Prayer

Lesson:

Diwali is the Hindu festival of lights celebrated in India during the fall new moon. During the dark nights of the new moon, people gather to light lights and to celebrate the return of Lord Rama. Thousands of years ago Rama was in exile, but returned after winning an epic war.

The festival of Diwali lasts nearly one week and is a time for shopping, eating, gift-giving, and great celebration. It represents both a new fiscal year and the clearing and illuminating of the mind. Hundreds of oil diyas made from clay are lit in homes to create a festive, bright atmosphere. Firecrackers are set off to celebrate the festival.

Because this is a dark time of year, think of ways your family can create light in your home. Although kids may have a difficult time understanding inner-light, try explaining the importance of a glowing, loving heart. People in India light diyas to represent light that illuminates the heart, mind, and body.

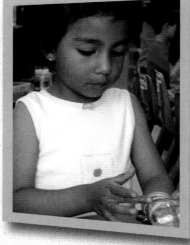

Project: Candle Holder

Cut small pieces of colored tissue paper. Glue the small pieces onto a glass jar. If the pieces overlap, new colors are created, which makes an even more interesting candle-holder. Place a candle in the middle of the jar and light at night (word of caution...don't light it near anything flammable and don't forget to blow it out).

Another variation is to mix one cup of flour with one cup of table salt and add just enough water to create a firm dough. Have the kids mold a clay pot, which you can bake and then paint. A candle can be placed in the homemade diya.

Closing: Blessing/Song/Prayer

Screaming
Skeletons

Remembrance

Season:	Fall
Time:	45 minutes-1 hour
Country/Religion:	Mexico
Age:	3-14

Materials:
white paper
construction paper
scissors/glue
markers/crayons
paper towel rolls cut into 1 inch pieces

Theme: Prayer
Remembrance

Opening: Blessing/Song/Prayer

Lesson:

Mexicans celebrate the Day of the Dead on November 2. Originally celebrated for three days, the Day of the Dead combines All Soul's Day and All Saint's Day. It started as an ancient Aztec celebration and is a festive time to remember ancestors and loved ones.

People visit cemeteries bringing flowers, candles, pictures, and special foods. Costumes and sugar candies are created to look like skeletons doing silly things. Rather than being scary, the skeletons represent activities the loved ones enjoyed while alive. Skeletons, for example, may be skateboarding, reading, dancing, or swimming. In Mexico, the skeletons are not feared, but rather, remembered fondly. The Day of the Dead is a time to celebrate life and to remember loved ones.

Read a story or search the Internet about the Day of the Dead. Discuss what it is and how people celebrate and remember loved ones. Talk about people you know who have died, and ask your kids how they can be remembered. Discuss dying in a way best suited for your family. Concentrate on remembering positive images of the people who have passed. If your children don't know of anyone who has died, talk about a famous president or someone they might recognize who has passed away.

Project: Silly Skeletons

Draw skeletons doing silly things. Cut them out and glue them onto one end of a paper towel roll that has been cut one inch high. Glue the other end of the paper towel roll to the colored paper so the skeletons appear 3-D

Closing: Blessing/Song/Prayer

Notes

Notes

Winter Playshops

Section Two: Winter

The Golden Rule

Universal belief: Do Unto Others as You Would Have Them Do Unto You

Season: Winter
Time: 45 minutes-1 hour
Country/Religion: Global
Age: 3-14

Materials: black paper
                     gold glitter/sequins
                     glue

Theme: The Golden Rule
        Tolerance
        Respect

Opening: Blessing/Song/Prayer

Lesson:

All five major world religions follow the Golden Rule. Thinking about yourself and how you would or would not want to be treated creates empathy for someone else. This global sense of community leads to peace. It is the most common and important underlying theme among different faiths. In his book, *Oneness*, Jeffrey Moses outlines the Golden Rule for each major religion:

> Hinduism: Do nothing to your neighbor, which hereafter, thou wouldst not have thy neighbor do to thee. Treat others, as thou wouldst thyself be treated.
>
> Buddhism: Hurt not others with that which pains yourself.
>
> Judaism: What is hurtful to yourself, do not to your fellow man.
>
> Christianity: Do unto others as you would have them do unto you.
>
> Islam: Do unto all men as you would they should unto you, and reject for others what you would reject for yourself.

Discuss what the Golden Rule means and why it is so important. Explain that while people may believe in different religions, there are many shared beliefs. Ask your children to give examples of how they would and would not like to be treated, and encourage them to follow the Golden Rule.

Project: Golden Art

Squeeze a bottle of glue and write (or drizzle) the Golden Rule on black paper. Cover the glue with gold glitter or gold sequins. Shake off excess glitter when you are finished and let dry. Place it in a prominent place for everyone in the family to read daily.

Closing: Blessing/Song/Prayer

Brilliant Benevolence

Christianity: Christmas/Epiphany

Season: Winter
Time: 45 minutes-1 hour
Country/Religion: Christianity
Age: 2-11

Materials: glass jar
                    construction paper
                    scissors
                    glue/tape
                    markers/crayons

Theme: Giving and sharing
Christmas/Epiphany
Charity

Opening: Sing "The Twelve Days of Christmas"

Lesson:

Many kids can tell you the story of baby Jesus lying in a manger. However, not all children understand the story of the Epiphany. The legend suggests three kings traveled across the Middle East, following the night sky. Seeking the baby Jesus, they spent twelve days reaching Bethlehem. They brought gold, frankincense, and myrrh as gifts for the baby, who they believed to be a great king sent from God.

Today, the Epiphany is celebrated on January 6 as the twelfth day of Christmas. The word epiphany means to reveal or to make known. The wise men revealed Jesus to the world.

The Christmas tradition of gift-giving started with the legend of the three kings. Use this lesson as an opportunity to talk about gift-giving. How does it make you feel when you give and receive? Does the size and quantity of a gift matter to you? How can kids help people who don't receive gifts? This is a great time of year to develop good-will and a sense of charity.

Project: Chore and Charity Jar

Cover an empty glass jar with small strips of construction paper and decorate. Cut out stars from yellow paper and glue them on to represent the night sky. Write twelve different chores on small slips of paper and put them in the jar. Every day ask a child to pick out a piece of paper, do the chore, and then replace the paper with a coin. The jar will begin to jingle as it fills. On the Epiphany go shopping to buy gifts of food for the needy.

Closing: Sing "We Three Kings of Orient Are"

Power of Heart

The importance of leading from one's heart

Season: Winter
Time: 45 minutes-1 hour
Country/Religion: Global
Age: 3-14

Materials: construction paper
                           sand paper
                           glue/scissors
                           crayons
                           white paper

Theme: Love
Self-esteem
Sharing
Support of God/Spirit

Opening: Blessing/Song/Prayer

Lesson:

Because Valentine's Day falls on February 14, this winter Playshop focuses on one's heart and the meaning of love. Sometimes children feel left out or sad that they don't receive valentines at school. This Playshop helps remind them of loved ones in their life, and of the unseen love of God.

Talk with your kids about what love means. Ask your kids to name some of the people they love, and who love them. Write the names on a piece of paper. Add to the list God, the Great Spirit, Allah, or whomever it is your children believe in. Remind them one cannot see God, just like you cannot see your own heart. You cannot "see" love, but you know what love is.

Explain that we hold love in our hearts, and it is our heart that keeps us alive. Our heart, with God in it, should lead us. Remind children that when they are lonely or sad (you can ask them to share an experience), our hearts remind us of love, even when it's not easy to see.

Project: Heart Art

Trace a heart on a piece of sand paper and cut it out. Place a sheet of white paper on top of the heart. Ask your children to color on top of the white paper, revealing the sand paper beneath. Explain that the sandpaper is like God in our hearts: full of texture and support but unable to be seen. Glue the piece of paper that reveals the heart onto a larger piece of construction paper. Write names of loved ones around the border.

Closing: Blessing/Song/Prayer

Ramadan Revelry

Celebrating Ramadan joyfully

Season:	Winter
Time:	45 minutes-1 hour
Country/Religion:	Islam
Age:	3-18
Materials:	a roll of shelf paper
	markers
	tablecloth
	food for a feast

Theme: Ramadan
Prayer
Self-control and obedience
Respect

Opening: Blessing/Song/Prayer

Lesson:

People who celebrate the religion of Islam are Muslims. Islam is an Abrahamic religion, and Muslims honor both Jewish and Christian biblical figures as great prophets. However, they believe Mohammad was given direct revelation from God, or Allah, in order to set straight earlier misinterpretations of God's meaning. The revelations are written in the Muslim holy book, the Qur'an. Mohammad's revelation is remembered during the month of Ramadan.

Ramadan is the ninth month of the Muslim calendar. Muslims believe the angel Gabriel (Jibral) directed the revelations from Allah on the 27th night of Ramadan. This night, Lailatul Qudr, is referred to as the night of power and is considered the most sacred night of the year.

The month of Ramadan is an intense period when Muslims engage in prayer and fast. A meal may be eaten before dawn, nothing is eaten or drunk all day, and then once the sun sets, a large feast is prepared. The nights during Ramadan are spent with family feasting, and celebrating their faith.

Project: Table Runner and Feast

Talk about what it would be like not to eat all day. How does one feel without eating or drinking? Remind children to respect Muslims in their community who are fasting for Ramadan.

Ask children what they might want to eat after a day with no food. Plan a feast together including some of their choices. Place the food on a tablecloth with a runner made of white shelf paper across the table. Have the kids decorate the runner with their own drawings of things they pray to God about. Enjoy a family feast together.

Closing: Blessing/Song/Prayer

Giant Attack

Judeo-Christian Story:
David and Goliath

Season:	Winter
Time:	45 minutes-1 hour
Country/Religion:	Judaism, Christianity
Age:	3-11

Materials:	Bible
	cardboard
	scissors
	glue
	markers/crayons
	empty cardboard roll of wrapping paper
	foil
	yarn

Theme: Faith
Trust
Courage
Overcome bullying

Opening: Blessing/Song/Prayer

Lesson:

The Hebrew Bible is referred to many as the Old Testament. It is a shared collection of lessons, stories, psalms, history, and prophecy, which both Jews and Christians believe to be holy. The story of David and Goliath takes place during a time when the Israelites were at war with the Philistines. Goliath, rumored to be a giant for his time, challenged anyone to a fight. None accepted, until a small shepherd boy, David, rose to the occasion. He believed in himself, in his heart, and in God. In one shot, he killed Goliath with a stone from his slingshot. David later became a great king.

Read the story directly from the Old Testament, so that children can hear the language of the time. Discuss what happened to David. Was he afraid or did he believe in himself? Who helped him? What was Goliath like? After talking about the story ask your children if anything similar has happened to them. Have they ever been bullied? Were they ever afraid of something or someone? What can they do to feel strong and courageous? This kind of conversation opens dialogue about friends who sometimes disappoint us, about bullies, and about support systems (God, family, other friends).

Project: Swords and Shields

Draw the outline of a shield on a piece of cardboard. Cut it out and decorate with scraps of paper, markers, paint, or glitter. Use a hole-punch to create two holes at the top…one on each side of the shield. Tie a piece of long string (30 inches) through one hole and tie the other end of the string through the other hole so the shield can hang from one's neck. Wrap a cardboard paper roll in foil to make a sword (a substitute for a slingshot). Once the swords and shields are ready, set some rules for a romp (no poking in the eye, no stabbing a baby sister too hard, etc.). One parent can act the role of Goliath while one child pretends to be David. Take turns if there is more than one child. Engage with heart!

Closing: Prayer asking for faith and trust in God, and in yourself.

Notes

Notes

Spring

Section Three: Spring

Vesak Vase

Buddha's birthday

Season: Spring
Time: 45 minutes-1 hour
Country/Religion: Buddhism
Age: 3-14

Materials: tissue paper
                    yarn
                    tape/scissors
                    plastic butter lids
                    yogurt lids

Theme: Compassion
Enlightenment
Creation/life cycles
Meditation

Opening: Blessing/Song/Prayer

Lesson:

Vesak is a day that celebrates Buddha's birth, life, his enlightenment, and his death. It is considered one of the most important holidays in Buddhism. People spend the day feasting, meditating, and rejoicing. Vesak is also referred to as Wesak, Visakha, and the Buddha Day. It is usually celebrated during the last two weeks of May.

Buddhism began in India. Legend has it that a sage prophesied that a young prince, Siddhartha Gautama, would one day become a great spiritual leader. When Siddhartha's parents heard the prophesy they tried to protect him from the world by building a large wall around the palace. Eventually Siddhartha chose to leave. Dismayed by the great poverty and suffering he witnessed, Siddhartha renounced his wealthy inheritance and began a meditation practice of his own. His practice merged the mindfulness of body and mind until he reached enlightenment and became the Buddha.

The lotus flower is a Buddhist symbol resembling the continuous life flow, and is often shared during Vesak in honor of the Buddha's life, death, and enlightenment. Lotus flowers grow in the mud and emerge as elegant flowers. Buddhists believe that life can begin with an ordinary person, who may have a muddy background, but who can become an elegant being.

Project: Flower Garlands

Trace a butter container lid on a piece of tissue paper. Trace a lid from a smaller yogurt container on a different colored piece of tissue paper. Cut out both circles on the traced lines. Place the smaller circle on top of the larger circle. Pinch the center of the circles together and twist to create a small stem. The circles should fold up a bit to resemble a flower. Older children can cut wavy lines around the edges of the circles to make them fancier. Do many variations of colors and flowers. Cut a piece of yarn about three feet long and tie around the "stems" of the flower to create a garland.

Closing: Blessing/Song/Prayer

Mind the Matzoh

Learning about Pesach

Season:	Spring
Time:	45 minutes-1 hour
Country/Religion:	Judaism
Age:	2-18

Materials: paper plate
egg, salt water
Haggadah
apple, nuts, sugar, grape juice
lamb shank or chicken wing
parsley

Theme: Grace
Faith
Passover

Opening: Blessing/Song/Prayer

Lesson:

Passover is a time to remember the heritage and legacy of the Jewish people during their enslavement in Egypt thousands of years ago. In order to convince the Pharaoh to release the Jews, Yahweh (God) delivered a series of plagues to the Egyptians. The final plague was the death of the firstborn boy in every family. However, Jews were warned ahead of time, and marked their homes so that the angels delivering the plague would pass over their homes. The name Passover comes from this "passing over."

Today, Jewish families gather for Pesach (Passover) and rejoice with a special dinner called a Seder. Everyone at the table gets a chance to read the Passover story from a Haggadah. As the story is told, certain foods are served that represent aspects of the story. A Seder plate is set aside with ingredients that represent the meanings of Pesach. Herbs rest on the plate to remind Jews of their bitter days as slaves. A lamb shank represents offerings to God, and an egg represents the festival offering of ancient times. Charoses, a mixture of apples, cinnamon, and nuts, resembles the mortar used to build cities, and the salt water reminds Jews of their ancestors' tears. On a different plate Jews place matzoh, or unleavened bread, to remember how quickly they had to flee from the Pharaoh's wrath. Both during and after the meal everyone reclines and celebrates their freedom from slavery.

Project: Seder Plate

Have the kids color pictures on a paper plate of the five important parts of the Seder dinner. Host your own Passover. Go to a local library or search the Internet for Jewish recipes and traditions. You can substitute a chicken wing for a lamb shank to make it kid-friendly. Read through a Haggadah. Celebrate and sing!

Closing: Blessing/Song/Prayer

Eggs, Eggs, Eggs

Easter eggs, spiritual eggs

Season: Spring
Time: 45 minutes-1 hour
Country/Religion: Christianity
Age: 3-14

Materials: hard boiled eggs
                       dye
                       glue
                       cardboard
                       marker/pen

Theme: Life and renewal
Easter
Symbols

Opening: Blessing/Song/Prayer

Lesson:

Christians celebrate Easter in the spring, commemorating the resurrection of Jesus as the son of God. Jesus, a Jewish teacher and social activist, was sentenced to die by the ruling Roman Empire two thousand years ago. Jesus was crucified, a form of execution by which a person was nailed to a cross and left to die. Christians believe Jesus rose from the dead on the third day. Sunday, the day he was resurrected, now serves as a Christian holy day, and a cross is the most common Christian symbol.

The theme of new life and renewal is celebrated in many ways and often symbolized by the Easter egg. An egg represents a new life, both literally and spiritually. Eggs are painted in vibrant spring colors as a sign of new life and the resurrection of Jesus. This Playshop is a good time to discuss the importance and use of symbols in religions and culture.

Project: Egg Shell Mosaic

Draw a simple picture on a piece of cardboard. Dip hard boiled eggs in dye or food coloring. After they dry, peel the eggs (let the kids eat them!), and use pieces of the shell to glue onto their cardboard pictures. The picture will become a mosaic made of Easter egg shells.

Closing: Blessing/Song/Prayer

Meditating Moments

Understanding the power of quiet moments

Season:	Spring
Time:	45 minutes-1 hour
Country/Religion:	Global
Age:	3-18
Materials:	construction paper
	white paper
	glue
	markers/crayons
	pillows

Theme: Peace
Nature
Meditation
Creativity

Opening: Blessing/Song/Prayer

Lesson:

Meditation is a practice used in different faiths. Some religions call it prayer, while others call it yoga, breathing exercise, or mindfulness. Setting time to devote to God or the Great Divine is a universal ritual.

Meditation creates a space to quiet one's mind and to become more aware of spirituality and a sense of peace. During meditation some people reflect on important issues, others remember significant people in their lives, and many focus on a thought, place, or symbol while trying to quiet their mind. Meditation takes a person away from the chaos of regular routines, and creates a sense of peace. Most importantly, meditation or prayer develops communication with God and a universal spirit.

Project: Meditation

Ask your kids to get very comfortable on their backs using pillows and blankets. Tell them to be quiet as they close their eyes. Play soothing music while you lead them through a meditation.

Sample meditation: "Imagine sitting on a rock looking over the sea. Listen for waves and birds. Look at the clouds moving across the sky. Notice an animal (kids may choose what kind) coming to visit. Watch the animal. Listen. Talk to the animal. Slowly open your eyes and sit up."

Ask your children to draw what they saw. Glue their pictures on a larger piece of construction paper as a frame. After they have made their artwork, move back into a circle and ask everyone to share. Talk about their different animals and about the nature they saw or felt. Ask them how they think God communicates. Each meditation is unique, just like our relationship to God.

Closing: Blessing/Song/Prayer

Mosaic Madness

Discovering Islamic architecture

Season: Spring
Time: 45 minutes-1 hour
Country/Religion: Islam
Age: 3-16

Materials: cardboard
                    colored paper scraps
                    glue/scissors
                    markers/crayons

Theme: Islamic architecture
Places of worship
Tolerance
Prayer
Geography

Opening: Blessing/Song/Prayer

Lesson:

Islam is growing faster than any other world religion. Spin a globe and find countries with large Muslim populations: most of the Middle East and large parts of Africa and Southeast Asia are Islamic countries.

A mosque is a building where Muslims go to pray. The holy day for Muslims is Friday. The architecture of a mosque usually includes an open courtyard and two tall towers resembling gates to heaven, called minarets. The towers were originally used as watch towers. Many mosques are decorated with mosaic designs that explain stories about the culture and religion of Islam. Visit a real mosque in your community or look up pictures of one on the Internet.

Teach your kids how a mosque looks different from your own place of worship and make some comparisons. Discuss why people go to a place to worship. Talk about some of the different ways people pray.

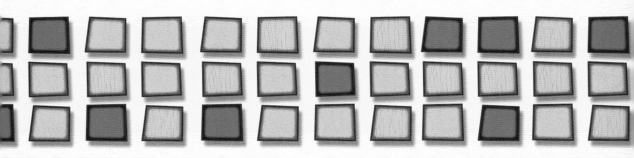

Project: Clay Mosaics

Have the kids design a simple drawing on a piece of cardboard. Roll out a piece of clay and cut it into small pieces. Bake the clay and paint the pieces when they are cooled. Glue the pieces of clay directly onto the cardboard design to create a mosaic. Leave white cracks between the pieces to look like the mortar in real mosaics. For older children you may want to break pieces of real pottery and lay them in plaster to create a mosaic.

Closing: Blessing/Song/Prayer

Notes

Notes

Summer Playshops

Section Four: Summer

Sister and Brother Bracelets

Hindu festival: Raksha Bandhan

Season: Summer
Time: 45 minutes-1 hour
Country/Religion: Hinduism
Age: 3-16

Materials: thread/yarn
                        beads
                        macaroni
                        glue
                        food coloring

Theme: Sibling bonds
Giving
Protection
Family
Geography

Opening: Blessing/Song/Prayer

Lesson:

The festival of Raksha Bandhan concentrates on family. It is a celebration of love and protection between brothers and sisters and is celebrated primarily in the Hindu country of India.

According to ancient tradition, a woman would tie a bracelet around a man's wrist to keep him safe during battle. In return the man would vow to protect the woman when he returned.

Today, Raksha Bandhan is a time to celebrate love and kinship between brothers and sisters. In India, children give candy and bracelets to their siblings, demonstrating their love and allegiance to each other. Rasksha translates to protection, and Bandhan means bonds or ties.

This is a good lesson to talk about protecting one another and creating special bonds in your family. You can compare gift-giving traditions in your own culture. Find India on a map and discuss the traditions of Hinduism.

Project: Bead Bracelets

Cut pieces of yarn, plastic string, or colored ribbons into 8-inch strips. Place a number of beads in front of each child. Let them string the beads. Put uncooked macaroni noodles in a plastic bag. Squirt a couple drops of food coloring in the bag and let the kids squeeze it around to color the macaroni. Dry the noodles on paper towels, and string them with the other beads. Older kids may be able to braid yarn or weave fancier bracelet designs. Create an informal ceremony for the kids to exchange their bracelets with each other.

Closing: Blessing/Song/Prayer

Native Knowledge

Introduction to Native American spirituality

Season:	Summer
Time:	45 minutes-1 hour
Country/Religion:	Native America
Age:	3-14
Materials:	poles/sticks/chairs
	blankets/cloth
	campfire
	sleeping bag/blankets
	simple foods

Theme: Nature
Faith
Cultural influences
Survival skills
Native American

Opening: Blessing/Song/Prayer

Lesson:

Native Americans are a diverse group of people with many different rich customs. Choose one or two tribes and explore their traditional life. As your kids learn about their culture, ask them how the geography and climate play a role in their customs, lifestyle, food, and lodging.

Religion and spirituality differ between native cultures, but most revere aspects of nature and divinity. Often referred to as First Nations People as a term for ethnicity in Canada, four guidelines from the Great Spirit are followed:

1. Respect Mother Earth
2. Respect the Great Spirit
3. Respect fellow beings
4. Respect individual freedom

Invite a speaker or someone knowledgeable to come and tell stories and legends or use websites and libraries to find resources.

Project: Forts and Fun

Ask your kids to pretend they are Native Americans living a long time ago. Have them go outside and create a shelter, or let them use blankets and chairs to create an inside fort. Build a campfire...teaching appropriate safety skills. Talk about how they would get food if they lived outside. Go on a hike to see if they can find berries, acorns, or dandelion greens. Ask what they would wear and how they would make clothing. Prepare a simple meal for them to eat in their structure. Tell stories to entertain each other. Ask what they could do for fun without games, TV, or computers. Talk about how their "real" life is different from Native cultures living a century ago. Ask them how life was harder or easier, and why faith was important. If you can, visit a reservation.

Closing: Blessing/Song/Prayer

Money Matters

Finance, charity, responsibility

Season:	Summer
Time:	45 minutes-1 hour
Country/Religion:	Global
Age:	3-14
Materials:	white paper
	construction paper
	scissors
	glue
	markers/crayons

Theme: Responsibility
Charity
Money
Saving

Opening: Blessing/Song/Prayer

Lesson:

Most religions discuss money, and all have provisions to help the poor. World religions proclaim the importance and responsibility of giving. Children see money used but don't always understand how it is earned or what to do with it. This Playshop is a good time to teach the value of earning money, saving it, spending, and contributing to charity.

Discuss how people can earn a living, develop savings, and contribute to the needy. Talk about what happens without money and how money can be lost. After a natural disaster organizations are looking for relief funds. Giving children a way to relieve others helps them process their own questions, creates empathy, and encourages responsibility. They can help someone in need and also save money for themselves.

Project: Box Banks

Cover a shoebox with wrapping paper or with plain white paper and decorate. Build two "walls" out of pieces of cardboard taped inside the box, splitting the box into thirds. Cut three slits in the lid, one over each section of the box. Give the kids a job to do and pay them 15 cents. Put one nickel in each slot. One section will become money they can spend, one section will be for savings, and one for charity.

Closing: Blessing/Song/Prayer

Sowing Seeds

Understanding parables

Season:	Summer
Time:	45 minutes-1 hour
Country/Religion:	Christianity
Age:	3-14
Materials:	Bible
	dirt
	paper cup
	mustard seeds

Theme: Faith
Listening
Compassion
Growth

Opening: Blessing/Song/Prayer

Lesson:

The teachings of Christianity are based on the teachings of Jesus. Jesus taught by example, by asking questions, and by sharing stories or parables. Parables are short narratives used to explain morals and ethics.

The parable of the mustard seed is a story Jesus told his twelve devoted followers, referred to as disciples. They traveled with Jesus as his students and then taught others what they learned. Sometimes, they wondered why they could not perform miracles or do some of the things Jesus could do. He answered by telling them that people needed faith the size of a mustard seed. A mustard seed is tiny, but grows in the most difficult conditions into a large tree. Faith grows.

In a different Bible verse Jesus explains that heaven is like a mustard seed. The seed grows and becomes a place of refuge for birds just like heaven is a place of refuge for faithful followers. Jesus used visual descriptions that his followers could understand and relate to. Parables help teach people about God and about faith.

Project: Grow a Garden

Read Matthew 13: 31-32 and 17: 19-20 in the Bible. Ask the kids about their thoughts on faith and what it means to them. Show them a mustard seed and let them plant it in a garden or even in a cup of dirt. Let them water and take care of it.

Closing: Blessing/Song/Prayer

Hiking Hajj

Islamic importance of the Hajj

Season:	Summer
Time:	45 minutes-1 hour
Country/Religion:	Islam
Age:	4-18
Materials:	walking shoes
	snacks
	a place to hike/walk
	journal/pen

Theme: Nature
Obedience
Prayer
Geography

Opening: Blessing/Song/Prayer

Lesson:

Islam maintains Five Pillars of Faith, which serve as behavioral guidelines for all Muslims.

1. Faith: there is no god but Allah, and Muhammad is his Prophet.
2. Prayer: five times a day in the direction of Mecca
3. Charity: two and one half percent of one's earnings should be given to the poor
4. Ramadan: the holy month of Islam when Muslims fast during the day
5. Pilgrimage: every Muslim who is able should journey to Mecca at least once in a lifetime

The last principle, the pilgrimage, is called a Hajj. Muslims travel to Saudi Arabia from all over the world to make a hajj to Mecca, Islam's most holy city. The Kaaba sits inside the Great Mosque where people come to pray. Muslims believe the Kaaba was built by Abraham and his son, Ishmael. No matter where Muslims live, they kneel facing the direction of Mecca and pray five times a day. Following the Pillars of Faith is crucial to a devout Muslim.

Find Saudi Arabia on a map. Look up pictures of Mecca on the computer or at a library. Discuss the importance of obedience for Muslims.

Project: Journal Journey

Ask your kids where they would like to pray. It could be their church or temple. It could be a serene spot in nature, or it could be a commercial building. Talk about why people pray. Ask your kids to prepare questions and thoughts about prayer. Walk to the place they have chosen to pray, and ask them to write their thoughts in their journal, or draw if they are young. Remind them about the journey Muslims make all the way to Mecca to pray.

Closing: Blessing/Song/Prayer

Notes

Notes

Appendix

Resources

Multicultural Books

Young Children
. . . .

Black Is Brown Is Tan; Adoff, A.
Amelia's Road; Altman, L. & Sanchez, E.
The Little Rabbit Who Wanted Red Wings; Bailey, C.S.
What is God?; Boritzer, E.
The Moccasin Goalie; Brownridge, W.
A Christmas Memory; Capote, T.
Do Princesses Wear Hiking Boots?; Coyle, C.L.
I'm Gonna Like Me; Curtis, J.L.
The Whispering Cloth; Deitzshea, P.
The Worry Stone; Dengler, M.
Diwali; Deshpande, C.
Uncle Willie and the Soup Kitchen; DiSalvo-Ryan, D.
Everybody Bakes Bread; Dooley, N.
God Is My Friend; Englehardt, L.
The Hundred Dresses; Estes, E.
The Day of Ahmed's Secret; Heide, F. & Gilliland, J.
Amazing Grace; Hoffman, M.
The Colors of Us; Katz, K.
Hershel and the Hanukkah Goblins; Kimmel, E. and Hyman, T.S.
Children Just Like Me; Kindersley, B. & Kindersley, A.
Gooney Bird Greene; Lowry, L.
Just the Way You Are; Lucado, M.
Through Grandpa's Eyes; MacLachlan, P.

Magrid Fasts for Ramadan; Matthews, M.
*Hands Around the World: 365 Creative Ways to Encourage Cultural Awareness and Global Respe*ct; Milford, S.
Tatterhood and the Hobgoblins; Mills, L.
Uncle Jed's Barbershop; Mitchell, M.K.
Light the Lights!: A Story About Celebrating Hanukkah & Christmas; Moorman, M.
Zen Shorts; Muth, J.
The Story of the Kind Wolf; Nicki, P.
Heather Has Two Mommies; Newman, L.
Angel Prayers; O'Keefe, S.H.
Dreamcatcher; Osofsky, A.
Seven Candles for Kwanzaa; Pinkney, A.
Hooray for You; Richmond, M.
Aunt Harriet's Underground Railroad in the Sky; Ringgold, F.
The Best Christmas Pageant Ever; Robinson, B.
Bless Us All; Rylant, C.
The Jester has Lost His Jingle; Saltzman, D.
God's Paintbrush; Sasso, S.E.
Don't Laugh at Me; Seskin, S. & Shamblin, A.
Under the Moon; Sheldon, D.
Why Am I Different?; Simon, N.
Who's in a Family?; Skutch, R.
Under the Rose Apple Tree; Thich Nhat Hanh
Annie...Anya a Month in Moscow; Trivas, I.
Ruby's Wish; Yim, S.
William's Doll; Zolotow, C.

Older Youth
· · · · · · · · · · ·

How the Garcia Girls Lost their Accents; Alvarez, J.
Journey of the Sparrows; Buss, L.
Silent Dancing; Cofer, J.
The Watsons Go to Birmingham-1963; Curtis, C.
Because of Winn-Dixie; Dicamillo, K.
The Hundred Dresses; Estes, E.
The Voice that Challenged a Nation: Marian Anderson and the Struggle for Equal Rights; Freedman, R.

The Curious Incident of the Dog in the Night-time; Haddon, M.
Hoot; Hiaasen, C.
Rumble Fish; Hinton, S.E.
When Hitler Stole Pink Rabbit; Kerr, J.
Kira-Kira; Kadohata, C.
To Kill A Mockingbird; Lee, H.
Gooney Bird Greene; Lowry, L.
One Fat Summer; Lipsyte, R.
The Girl-Son; Neuberger, A.
Cry, the Beloved Country; Paton, A.
Criss Cross; Perkins, L.R.
Keeping You a Secret; Peters, J.A.
The Chosen; Potok, C.
Maniac Magee; Spinelli, J.
The Cay; Taylor, T.
Huckleberry Finn; Twain, M.
Bread Givers; Yezierska, A.
Be a Friend: Children Who Live with HIV Speak; Wierner, L.S. & Best, A.

Adults
· · · · · · ·

The House of the Spirits; Allende, I.
How the Garcia Girls Lost their Accents; Alvarez, J.
10 Little Indians; Alexie, S.
Aman; Barnes, V.L. & Buddy, J.
Expecting Adam; Beck, M.
Natasha; Bezmozgis, D.
Dr. Zhivago; Boris, P.
Bury My Heart at Wounded Knee; Brown, D.
The Good Earth; Buck, P.
May You Be the Mother of a Hundred Sons; Bumiller, E.
Waiting for Snow in Havana; Carlos, E.
Blood Brothers; Chacour, E.
Wild Swans; Chang, J.
Silent Dancing; Cofer, J.
Lakota Woman; Crow Dog, M.

Power of One; Courtenay, B.
A Tale of Two Cities; Dickens, C.
A Yellow Raft in Blue Water; Dorris, M. S.; Drakulic, S.
Like Water for Chocolate; Esquivel, L.
Middlesex; Eugenides, J.
One Thousand White Women; Fergus, J.
White Oleander; Fitch, J.
The Women's Room; French, M.
A Passage to India; Forester, E.M.
The World Is Flat; Friedman, T.
From Beirut to Jerusalem; Friedman, T.
A Lesson Before Dying; Gaines, E.
100 Years of Solitude; Garcia Marquez, G.
Memoirs of a Geisha; Golden, A.
Snow Falling on Cedars; Guterson, D.
War Trash; Ha Jin
The Way of all Women; Harding, M.
Chocolat; Harris, J.
Baghadad Without a Map; Horwitz, T.
The Kite Runner; Hosseini, K.
Les Miserables; Hugo, V.
Their Eyes Were Watching God; Hurston, Z.N.
Dancing with the Witchdoctor; James, K.
Geography of the Heart; Johnson, F.
Gate of the Sun; Khoury, E.
The Poisonwood Bible; Kingsolver, B.
Amazing Grace; Kozel, J.
The Namesake; Lahiri, J.
To Kill a Mockingbird; Lee, H.
The Color of Water; McBride, J.
Angela's Ashes; McCourt, F.
The PeaceFinder; McWilliams, J.
Palace Walk; Mahfouz, N.
The Ladies Auxilary; Mirvis, T.
Confessions of a Mask; Mishima, Y.
A Fine Balance; Mistry, R.
Song of Solomon; Morrison, T.

The True Story of Hansel and Gretel; Murphy, L.
A Few Short Notes on Tropical Butterflies; Murray, J.
The Women of Brewster Place; Naylor, G.
Black Elk Speaks; Neihardt, J.
Milagro Beanfield War; Nichols, J.
Drinking Coffee Elsewhere; Packer, Z.Z.
Snow; Pamuk, O.
Black and Blue; Quindlen, A.
The God of Small Things; Roy, A.
Midnight's Children; Rushdie, S.
Princess; Sasson, J.
Grapes of Wrath; Steinbeck, J.
The Bookseller of Kabul; Seirestad, A.
A Tree Grows in Brooklyn; Smith, B.
Sophie's Choice; Styron, W.
The Joy Luck Club; Tan, A.
The Haj and Trinity; Uris, L.
Rain of Gold; Villasenor, V.
Possessing the Secret of Joy; Walker, A.
Night; Wiesel, E.
Native Son; Wright, R.

Religious Books and Resources

Hinduism
· · · · · · · · ·

Bhagavad-Gita
Upanishads
Mahabharata
Ramayana
The Vedas
Puranas
Yoga Philosophy of Patanjali; Aranya, H. S.
The Breath of God; Chinmayananda, S.
The Way to God; Ghandi, M.
An Introduction to Hinduism; Flood, G.

Daughters of the Goddess: The Women Saints of India; Johnsen, L.
Hinduism: A Very Short Introduction; Knott, K.
Hindu Culture; Tejomayananda. S.
An Autobiography of a Yogi; Yogananda, P.

www.hindueducation.org
www.Hindunet.org
www.Hindulinks.org
www.hinduism.co.za
www.balagokulam.org

Buddhism

Books by the Dalai Lama
Books by Thich Nhat Hanh
Buddha; Armstrong, K.
The Places that Scare You; Chodron, P.
Thoughts Without a Thinker; Epstein, M.
The Story of Buddhism: A Concise Guide to its History and Teachings; Lopez, D.
Essential Buddhism: A Complete Guide to Beliefs and Practices; Maguire, J.
What the Buddha Taught; Rahula, W.
The Everything Buddhism Book; Sach, J.
The Buddhist Handbook; Snelling, J.

www.buddhanet.net
www.tricycle.com
www.buddha101.com
www.buddhaweb.org
www.buddhismtoday.com
www.dharmanet.org

Judaism

The Hebrew Bible: The Old Testament
The Essence of Judaism; Baeck, L.

The Power of Kabbalah; Berg, Y.
The Five Books of Moses for Young People; Cassway, E.
*Living a Jewish Life: Jewish Traditions, Customs, and Values for
Today's Families*; Diamant, A. & Cooper, C.
The Left Hand of God; Lerner, M.
Essential Judaism: A Complete Guide to Beliefs, Customs, and Rituals; Robinson, G.
This Is My God: The Jewish Way of Life; Wouk, H.

www.ajc.org
www.jewishfamily.com
www.caje.org
www.shamash.org
www.joi.org
www.snj.com/jhen
www.myjewishlearning.com

Christianity

Bible
World Christian Encyclopedia
Eerdmans' Handbook to the History of Christianity
Godly Play; Berryman, J.
The Heart of Christianity; Borg, M.
Understanding the Bible; Buehrens, J.
The Coming of the Cosmic Christ; Fox, M.
The Good Book; Gomes, P.
If Grace Is True; Gulley, P. and Mulholland, J.
Traveling Mercies; Lamott, A.
The Four Loves; Lewis, C.S.
Reconstructing Christianity; Mayfield, R.
Beyond Belief; Pagels, E.
The Soul of Christianity; Smith, H.
God's Politics; Wallis, J.

www.wcc-coe.org
www.tcpc.org
www.commonsensechristianity.org

Islam
• • • • • •

Qur'an
Haddith
A Border Passage; Ahmed, L.
The Everything Koran Book; Anwar, D.
Muhammad; Armstrong, K.
What Everyone Needs to Know About Islam; Esposito, J.
Muhammad Is His Messenger; Schimmel, A.
Books by Naguib Mafouz
Books by Fatima Mernissi
Books by W. Montgomery Watt

www.cie.org
www.islamicity.com
www.iiie.net
www.islam.com
www.islam-guide.com
islam.about.com

World Religions and Spirituality: General
• •

A Woman's Journey to God; Borysenko, J.
How to Negotiate With Kids...Even When You Think You Shouldn't; Brown, S.
How to Teach Peace to Children; Byler, A.M.
The Power of Myth; Campbell, J.
The History of Religion; Farrington, K.
The Soul of the Child; Gurian, M.
National Geographic Geography of Religion: Where God Lives, Where Pilgrims Walk;
Hitchcock, Tyler, and Esposito
The Faith Club; Idliby, R., Oliver, S., Warner, P.
Living Your Yoga: Finding the Spiritual in Everyday Life; Lasater, J.

God's Breath: Sacred Scriptures of the World; Miller, J. & Kenedi, A.
World Religions: From Ancient History to the Present; Parrinder, G.
Abounding Grace; Peck, S.
The Illustrated World's Religions: A Guide to Our Wisdom Traditions; Smith, H.
The World's Religions; Smith, H.
Oneness; Moses, J.
Living Simply with Children; Sherlock, M.
A World in Transition; Yogananda, P.
The Soul Would Have No Rainbow if the Eyes Had No Tears; Zona, G.
The Seat of the Soul; Zukov, G.

www.adherents.com
www.religioustolerance.org
www.InterfaithAlliance.org
www.pluralism.org
www.beliefnet.com
www.experiencefestival.com
www.tolerance.org
www.wikipedia.com
www.uri.org
www.explorefaith.org

World Music

Africa
· · · · · ·

So Kalmery: Congo
Ladysmith Black Mambazo
Thomas Mapfumo: Mozambique, Zimbabwe
Ex Centric Sound System: Trinidad and Tobago world fusion

Middle East
· · · · · · · · · · ·

Jihad Racy
Leo Fuld: Israel

Hossam Ramzy: Egypt
Essev Bar: Israel
Simon Shaheen: Palestine

Asia
· · · · ·

Choying Drolma and Steve Tibbetts: Tibet
Deben Bhattarcharya: Afghanistan, Tibet, Bangladesh
Liu Fang: China
Sevara Nazarkhan: Uzbekistan
Kitaro: Japanese-American
Karunesh: SE Asia
Kiran Ahluwalia: India

Australia
· · · · · · · ·

Bushfire: Aboriginal

Europe
· · · · · · ·

Michalis Terzis: Greek
Frigg: Scandinavia
The Clancy Brothers: Ireland
The King's College Choir: United Kingdom
Catherin Pfeifer: Germany
Dunvant Male Choir: Wales

North America
· · · · · · · · · · · ·

Burning Spear: Jamaican reggae
Los Camperos de Valles: Mexico

Gathering of Shamen: Native American
R. Carlos Nakai: Native American
Natalie MacMaster: Canada

South America
· · · · · · · · · · · · ·

Susana Baca: Peru
Brazilian Carnival: Brazil
Charanga Cakewalk: Columbia
Huracan De Fuego: Venezuela

Movies

(older youth and adults)

Amilie
Ben-Hur
Bend It Like Beckham
Billy Elliot
Born on the Fourth of July
Bowling for Columbine
Boys Don't Cry
The Bridge on the River Kwai
Brokeback Mountain
The Color Purple
Crash
Dances With Wolves
Do the Right Thing
El Norte
Empire of the Sun
Frida
That's a Family
Gandhi
The God's Must be Crazy
The Good Earth

Guess Who's Coming to Dinner
Hoop Dreams
Hotel Rwanda
The Human Stain
Iron & Silk
It's Elementary
The Joy Luck Club
Kandahar
The Last Emperor
Lawrence of Arabia
Life Is Beautiful
The Manchurian Candidate
My Left Foot
North Country
Philadelphia
The Pianist
The Postman
Rabbit-Proof Fence
Reds
Roots
Schindler's List
Seven Years in Tibet
Snow Falling on Cedars
Stand and Deliver
Transamerica
Tsotsi
Whale Rider

Statistics

World Religions by population

(2005 from www.adherents.com)

Christianity	2.1 billion
Islam	1.3 billion
Secular/Non-religious	1.1 billion
Hinduism	900 million

Chinese traditional	394 million
Buddhism	376 million
Primal-inigenous	300 million
African traditional & Diasporic	100 million
Sikhism	23 million
Juche	19 million
Spiritism	15 million
Judaism	14 million
Baha'I	7 million
Jainism	4.2 million
Shinto	4 million
Cao Dai	4 million
Zoroastrianism	2.6 million
Tenrikyo	2 million
Neo-Paganism	1 million
Unitarian-Universalism	800 thousand
Rastafarianism	600 thousand
Scientology	500 thousand

Top Ten Organized Religions in the United States

Percent of USA Population
(2001 from www.adherents.com)

Christianity	76.5%
Judaism	1.3%
Islam	.5%
Buddhism	.5%
Hinduism	.4%
Unitarian Universalist	.3%
Wicca/Pagan/Druid	.1%
Spiritualist	.05%
Native American Religion	.05%
Baha'I	.04%

Notes

1. Mark Twain, *The Innocents Abroad.*

2. Michael Gurian, *The Soul of the Child: Nurturing the Divine Identity of Our Children* (New York: Atria Books, 2002).

3. Robert L. Kohls and John M. Knight, *Developing Intercultural Awareness: A Cross-Cultural Training Handbook*, Second Edition (Boston: Intercultural Press, Inc., 1994).

4. Fenton Johnson, *Keeping Faith: A Skeptic's Journey* (New York: Houghton Mifflin Company, 2003).

5. Lutheran Pastor Rich Mayfield, personal interview, 2006.

6. Marcus Borg, *Meeting Jesus Again for the First Time: the Historical Jesus and the Heart of Contemporary Faith* (HarperSanFrancisco, 1994) and *The Heart of Christianity: Rediscovering a Life of Faith, How We Can Be Passionate Believers Today* (HarperSanFrancisco, 2003).

7. Philip Gulley and James Mulholland, *If God Is Love: Rediscovering Grace in an Ungracious World* (HarperSanFrancisco, 2004).

8. Statistics from www.adherents.com

9. Source: www.pbs.org/itus/caughtinthecrossfire/arab_americans.html

10. Jeffrey Moses, *Oneness: Great Principles Shared by All Religions* (New York: Ballantine Books, 2002).

11. Martin Luther King Jr., Letter from Birmingham Jail, April 16, 1963.

12. Michael Lerner, *The Left Hand of God: Taking Back Our Country From the Religious Right* (HarperSanFrancisco, 2006).

The creation of Soul Sunday would not have been possible without the graphic design work of both Jennifer Lindstrom and Stacey Sattler.

About Jennifer...

Jennifer Lindstrom is an award-winning graphic designer with over fourteen years of experience. Her ability to conceptualize and develop high profile corporate event branding identities and web design campaigns has enabled corporations such as Texas Instruments and Hewlett Packard to build successful event brands. She also excels in the development and design of corporate identities and museum and exhibit display elements. Jennifer resides in Denver, Colorado with her family.

About Stacey…

Stacey Sattler has a Master's in Art Education and has been teaching elementary school art in Ohio for more than fifteen years. She never tires of fostering creativity and excitement in the art room. Once a jewelry designer and artistic quilter, Stacey is now active in the scrapbook design industry. She loves creating pages that tell her family's stories and sharing their photographs. Stacey is a designer for the scrapbook website www.twopeasinabucket.com and frequently contributes to Simple Scrapbooks Magazine. Stacey is married to Jason Eggerstorfer and they have four amazing children.